LEEDS METROPOL'T/

Managing Violence in the Workplace

Dr. Thomas Capozzoli
and
R. Steve McVey

S_L^t

St. Lucie Press
Delray Beach, Florida

TABLE OF CONTENTS

PREFACE

Today, many of us spend between 35 and 65% of our waking hours at work. We bring to work our needs and our hopes, our passions and our fears. We seek affiliation, status, growth, and fulfillment. For some people, though, the workplace is a frustrating, sometimes overwhelming environment, where individual goals seem incompatible with those of the organization. Growth and fulfillment seem to be thwarted by the immediate expediencies of production. Initiative and innovation are discouraged in favor of bureaucratic uniformity and the industrial engineer's process sheet. When an employee experiences what seems to be arbitrary and capricious treatment by management, and there is no means of grievance or redress, the employee often feels like a victim of injustice. In many cases, the employee may have brought ineffective life skills to the job in the first place, and therefore the situation was likely to develop at some point. When an employee has insufficient coping skills to either react or recover, the situation can readily deteriorate into a negative cause-and-effect spiral. In this process, the person begins to lose the support of co-workers. With the loss of status and affiliation, the employee feels helpless, hopeless, alienated, and alone. Some employees in this situation choose to strike back in righteous vengeance against their antagonist(s)—the managers and co-workers whom they believe have turned against them.

The above scenario of the disenchanted employee is one of the typologies dissected and discussed in this book. But there are other typologies—those involving the ex–employee and the nonemployee. Reasons range from frustration to rejection to greed. The average American workplace has become a dangerous place. The Bureau of Labor Statistics reports that there were 22,400 work-related assaults in 1992, and the 1992 National Crime Victimization Survey reported 667,978 incidents of violence in the workplace. A Northwestern National Life Insurance Company report of a 1993 study indicated that there were over 2 million physical attacks in 1992, 6 million threatened, and yet another 16 million harassed in the American workplace. In 1992 and 1993, over 1,000 people were killed in the workplace, according to the U.S. Bureau of Labor.

Is there any way to reduce these staggering numbers? Can employers screen out applicants who would be potentially dangerous employees? Can employers and co-workers be trained to recognize potentially dangerous behaviors, and can employers intervene to either expel employees exhibiting such behaviors or reclaim them through effective employee assistance programs? Is there any way for organizations to make it more difficult for a possible perpetrator of violence to succeed? Is it possible to reduce or limit the danger and destruction wrought by perpetrators? Is there any means by which organizations can positively manage the aftermath to limit the continuing effects of such crises? The answer to each of these questions is yes.

While we realize that each of the above subject areas could encompass an entire book, we cover each subject area with a prescriptive outline of critical considerations to sensitize crisis managers to the expanse of concerns to be considered when beginning to design a comprehensive crisis management plan in an organization.

We welcome any comments, criticisms, or suggestions that readers might wish to offer which could be incorporated into revisions of this work or into future related works. Please correspond with us at: The National Center for the Management of Workplace Violence (NCMWV), P.O. Box 48, Westfield, IN 46074.

Steve McVey
Tom Capozzoli

ACKNOWLEDGMENTS

We would like to thank our wives, Susan Capozzoli and Jackie McVey, for their support and for editing our "stream of thought." Thanks also to our friend Bonnie Mitchell for her help in editing the manuscript.

THE AUTHORS

Dr. Thomas K. Capozzoli is an assistant professor of organizational leadership at Purdue University. He also is a senior consultant with Personnel Services, Inc., Carmel, Indiana, and a research associate in the National Center for the Management of Workplace Violence. Dr. Capozzoli spent 30 years with General Motors Corporation, retiring in 1992. During his time with GM, he was involved in management, labor relations, and internal consulting. It also was during this time that he became aware of and involved with violent acts in the workplace. He received a Doctorate in Education in 1987 from Ball State University.

R. Steve McVey is President and CEO of Personnel Services, Inc., Carmel Indiana, a management, human resources, and organizational development consulting firm. He also is an associate professor of organizational leadership at Purdue University and a research associate in the National Center for the Management of Workplace Violence. Prior to his teaching appointment, Professor McVey retired after 26 years as a Special Agent of the Federal Bureau of Investigation during which he was involved in the psychological analysis of a variety of violent criminal behaviors. He holds a Master of Public Administration degree from Baruch College of the City University of New York.

INTRODUCTION

Trigger Happy, A False Crisis:
How workplace violence became a hot issue.
Media Misinterpret Research,
Consultants Fuel Fears; Few Actually Go Postal

This was the headline of *The Wall Street Journal* on October 13, 1994. The article related how misinformed many executives and workers are about violence in today's workplace. The article contends that many of the homicides occurring in the workplace cannot legitimately be classified as "violence in the workplace" and that the chances of being killed by a disgruntled employee in the workplace are not very great.

Does the above article suggest that victims must be killed to make the event significant? Many are "only" assaulted, threatened, or harassed or have their property destroyed, but isn't that enough? Did the author of the above article interpret the statistics correctly? Is the author correct in asserting that workplace violence is not something we really need to worry about?

The Statistics

The U.S. Bureau of Labor Statistics has indicated that there were 1,062 work-related homicides in 1993 and that homicide was the second leading cause of death in the American workplace that year.

The National Crime Victimization Survey, U.S. Bureau of Labor Statistics, found that each year almost one million people become victims of crimes of violence at work. These crimes cost approximately 500,000 employees—and their employers—1,751,100 days of work and lost wages of at least $55 million. According to the U.S. Department of Justice, one in six violent crimes in the United States may happen at work, and nearly 8,000 workers have died on the job since 1980.

Joseph A. Kinney, National Safe Workplace Institute, has stated that between July 1992 and July 1993 one out of every four American workers was either harassed, threatened, or attacked.

A 1993 American Management Association survey found that one fifth of the companies polled reported that they had experienced workplace violence since 1990, and 8% of the organizations reported incidents resulting in death.

The Society for Human Resource Management reported that out of 479 human resource professionals surveyed, one third of them had witnessed at least one act of violence in their workplace since 1989, and 54% reported between two and five violent acts *since then.* Respondents reported that the violence had significantly affected employee morale, and 41% had noticed increased stress among their employees following a violent occurrence.

The National Institute for Occupational Safety and Health has reported that between 1980 and 1989 40% of women who died on the job were murdered and claims that homicide is the third overall leading cause of death in the workplace. Some experts now believe that the *leading* cause of death on the job for women is homicide.

Even if the above statistics are neither consistent nor exact, they still suggest that the *Wall Street Journal* article may be the one misleading American workers. Statistics are subject to significant interpretation and, taken alone, are generally inadequate grounds upon which to found truth. However, the principle of interocular trauma states that if one examines a set of data long enough, it will substantiate any assertion one wishes to make. The *Wall Street Journal* article minimized the assertions of the statistics. In this book, they are maximized. How many incidents of threats, intimidation, assault, and homicide does it take to constitute a "legitimate concern"?

Citizens place thousands of bets each day in state lotteries hoping to win against odds of one in 70 million. Statistics suggest that each of us has about a one-in-five chance of being a victim of some form of workplace violence *this year*! But does anyone consider the realities of either of those odds?

From all indications, the problem seems to be expanding. Whether or not the press wishes to label it as an epidemic truly worthy of concern seems to be irrelevant. With at least a minimum of 100,000+ incidents per year, it is a legitimate concern to both employees and employers.

"Safe Workplace" and "Reasonable Care" Doctrines

The U.S. Occupational Safety and Health Administration Act requires employers to "provide a safe workplace" for employees. Litigation flowing from the old common-law doctrine of master–servant liability has established the expectation by employees and the public that employers exercise "reasonable care" for their safety in the workplace and stand liable for wrongful acts of negligence by any employee. If an employer is found to have known, or should have known, that an employee was potentially likely to commit violence, that employer is liable for any subsequent acts committed by that employee in the workplace or anywhere else while in the service of that employer.

In the absence of definitive indicators as to when and where workplace violence will occur next, employers must develop procedures to reduce its potential. They must create contingency plans for actual events in order to fulfill their legal and moral obligations to their employees and to the public.

1

CASE EXAMPLES OF WORKPLACE VIOLENCE

Violence at Delco Remy

When one of the authors arrived on the scene in the parking lot of Delco Remy in Anderson, Indiana, a woman was lying face down and motionless on the pavement. There was a pool of blood near her head, and she had both hands pressed to the back of her head. There was a large crowd gathered, and he heard one of the security officers say he had called 911. As the author talked with witnesses, he learned that the woman had been shot in the back of the head by her ex-husband. The ex-husband had approached her as she left the plant at the end of her night shift, indicating he wanted "to talk to her." During the conversation, he became enraged, drew a small caliber gun, shot her, and fled. Fortunately, because of the small caliber of the bullet, the woman recovered.

That incident was more than 20 years ago, and the author can still vividly recall what transpired that night and the sight of the woman lying in blood on the parking lot pavement. Was that woman in the parking lot the only victim that night? If this had such a profound effect upon the author that he remembers it vividly 20 years later, how many others who were there that night remember that event as they cross that parking lot each night at the end of their shifts?

Was that the author's first exposure to workplace violence? Before that night, his experience with violence in the workplace had been limited to what he considered "minor" altercations between employees and/or management. Were these incidents "minor" because no one had been shot? For instance, a supervisor had once been beaten by an employee who had returned to work after lunch under the influence of alcohol. Various threats against supervisors by workers (too often dismissed as being just "part of the job"), fights between employees, and acts of vandalism to employees' and/or managers' personal properties had been fairly commonplace.

In another instance, an employee, who was never identified, threw a manufactured part at the head of a supervisor. The part barely missed him, but had it struck its mark, the supervisor would have been very seriously injured or killed. It was apparent that this incident created fear in the other supervisors, because each of them knew how easily it could have happened, or might yet happen, to them. Needless to say, it made quite an impression upon the intended victim, who recently remarked that he still recalls the event clearly after so many years.

In reflecting upon the number of such incidents, and the number of workers *and* managers recalled who appeared to have had emotional problems, the wonder is that there were not more such incidents resulting in serious injuries.

An Unexplained Shooting

Several years after the woman was shot at Delco Remy, another serious incident occurred at the same location. The author had just finished talking on the phone to

Randy, a co-worker, before going to a training session for plant supervisors. About one hour later, he was sitting in his office when the phone rang. It was Randy, and there was sheer terror in his voice. He said, "Cap, they shot the security guard and they are still shooting. I need help." He asked Randy where he was, and Randy quickly explained he was in the plant security office. In the background, the author could hear a popping noise that he assumed was gunfire. He instructed Randy to stay down and hang the phone up, and said he would call for help. He hung up and called 911 and the main security office. The main security office already had heard of the shooting and was already responding. A security guard had been critically wounded, and Randy was able to stay with him until medics arrived.

The security guard had been sitting in the office outside the plant when a man walked up. This in itself was not an unusual occurrence, but this man was carrying a shotgun. The security guard did not immediately see the gun. The man raised it, and before the guard could react he shot through the glass, wounding the guard. The guard did not know the man; no words were spoken. The assailant then fled.

By the time Randy called, there were no more shots being fired. What sounded like shots were actually pieces of glass falling from the shattered window and hitting the tile floor in the office. The assailant was from another division of the company. He had visited this particular plant regarding a product-related problem and, for some unexplained reason, returned to gun down the first person he saw there. The assailant was later killed in a shootout with police in another state. The security guard survived but was maimed for life.

The incident had a significant impact on many employees in the hours and days following the event, before the assailant was killed, even though they were not directly involved in the shooting. No one knew for certain who had done it, why, or if he would return to try it again. It seemed as if everyone was fearful, especially the other security guards in their offices in the front of each plant. They felt vulnerable to a similar attack. The shooting was *the* topic of conversation in every plant on every shift. Many work hours were spent discussing the incident, the assailant, his motive, and the likelihood that it would happen again.

It would be difficult to assess all of the losses this single incident cost the organization. The incident stirred more emotion than the parking lot shooting mentioned above. At least there was an explanation in the parking lot incident: a domestic problem. In this instance, there was no rational explanation, since the assailant was killed before he could be captured and questioned. His motive for returning to the plant to shoot the first person he saw was never determined. When reasons for an event are unknown, it makes the event appear to have been unpredictable, and therefore uncontrollable, intensifying the fears of even those employees not directly involved.

Both of the above events were looked upon as being isolated incidents, and neither made much news, even in the local media. The plant, of course, did not want the negative publicity and the effect it would have on the employees. Both incidents happened long before "violence in the workplace" had become an identifiable phenomenon.

Violence is occurring in all types of organizations, of all sizes and kinds. Although there are no reliable statistics indicating the exact costs of such incidents, the costs must be significant to the host organizations. Some of the related costs include suits alleging inability of the employer to provide a safe workplace or place of business, significant insurance payments for injuries, lower production by employees, and loss of business. Less obvious losses are continued loss of production by employees who are preoccupied by what happened to them or to fellow employees. Workers often take sides, even though not personally involved. Long after the incident is over, there may be residual effects in the loss of cohesion among workers whose cooperation is necessary for normal operations. If the principals in the incident are returned to work, there may be smoldering resentments and thoughts of revenge. Even if such tinder does not ignite into actual violence, such emotions and attitudes between employees create a continuing, negative undercurrent in the unit's operations.

The Chelsea School System: "Done Talking"

Chelsea, Michigan, is a small, quiet community near Ann Arbor. On December 16, 1993, a disgruntled Chelsea science teacher, 39-year-old Stephen Leith, shot and killed Superintendent Joseph Piasecki and wounded two other school officials. Just before the fatal encounter, Piasecki had received a telephone call from the bargaining representative for the Michigan Education Association warning him that Leith was on his way to Piasecki's office, possibly to harm him. Piasecki ignored the warning and denied he was in imminent danger. Twenty to thirty minutes after the warning call, Leith entered Piasecki's office with a 9-mm handgun and opened fire on him and the two other men with him.

After the shooting, Leith returned to his classroom, where he was arrested by the Chelsea chief of police. When arrested, Leith was calmly sitting at his desk with a stack of papers in front of him.

Leith had become angry and stormed out of an informal grievance meeting with Piasecki, a union steward, the school principal, and another teacher. The meeting concerned a second personnel file that Leith said the school district had been keeping on him and his behavior in school. Leith allegedly had been charged by a student with sexual harassment. Upon leaving the meeting, Leith went to another office where his wife, Alice, also a teacher, was and told her, "We're leaving." Alice's testimony in her husband's trial was recounted in the *Ann Arbor News* on August 6, 1994. According to Alice Leith, the following events occurred after they left the school:

> He was angry and peeled the car out of the lot ridiculously fast. I asked him to slow down, that he was scaring me. I told him when we got home we'd call an MEA representative and he said he was "done talking with people."
>
> When we got home, he poured me a cup of coffee and I started to make the call. The administration's secret file on Steve was open on the kitchen table and I pointed out to Steve one section. He looked at it and stiffened, went into a rigid stance. He said, "That's it! He's going to die!" He spun around and jogged upstairs in a very unnatural gait.

Alice Leith said she had reached the union representative's assistant on the phone and told her she was afraid that her husband might harm someone.

> When I hung up, Steve came down the stairs, and I didn't recognize him. His face was distorted, frozen, his expression was awful. If you'd saw (sic) anyone like that you'd be afraid. I told him "Steve, don't do this! Stay here with me." He looked right past me, brushed against me, and went out to his car. I didn't see a gun but I thought he might have one.
>
> I grabbed the file and thought if I could get to school we could work this out, even if we had to have a shouting match. I never thought of calling the police; I just wanted to get to school and stop it. I

drove out Liebeck Road as fast as I could but there was slow-moving traffic, school buses.

When I got to the school, I saw Steve walking along a walkway, his right hand in his pocket. I got out and followed him. I didn't call to him; there were people around and I didn't want to spook him. I went into the administration building thinking I could head him off. Then I heard multiple shots. I recognized what they were.

Alice Leith said she ignored warnings to leave the building. She entered Piasecki's office, where she encountered the disaster.

Joe (Piasecki) was lying on the floor, and Ron Meade was down. Steve had his back to me and turned around and pointed the gun at me. I didn't think he knew who I was. He was devoid of expression. I wondered if he was going to shoot me. I screamed, "What have you done?"

Phil Jones kept saying, "Steve, this is Alice, she loves you." I walked up to him and said, "Give me the gun," and he handed it to me. I put it on a table but then Steve got up from a chair like a zombie and picked up the gun from the table and left. I followed him, caught up with him, and reached in his jacket pocket and took the gun. I told him, "There's been enough killing." He said, "I'll be in my room. Go be with your friends." I put the gun under a desk and went back to the office to help.

The comments by students about Leith were mixed. According to the *Ann Arbor News*, some students said he was popular, friendly, funny, and often ate lunch with them. Some said he could relate to kids and fit in with them. With others, he was overly friendly and "aggressive." He was nominated several years in a row as one of Chelsea High's best teachers. However, he was known as a person who often butted heads with the school administration.

The years preceding the tragedy painted a dark picture of Stephen Leith. In the mid-1980s, Leith's chronic depression began to bring on suicidal tendencies, daily vomiting, violent fits of temper, periods of weeping, and boycotts of holiday celebrations. In one instance close to Christmas, Leith became very angry with his wife over her misquoting him in a phone conversation. He threatened to kill her and began running around outside their house. Leith's wife called the police. For her own safety, she spent the holidays with relatives in another city. Because of her husband's frequent fits of rage, she kept a bag packed in case she had to leave home suddenly.

During this time, Leith began to collect guns. When police searched the Leith home after the shootings, they found eight long guns, two handguns, and more than 2,000 rounds of ammunition. He let his usual neatly trimmed hair grow and fashioned it into a ponytail. He also began to kill small birds and animals in a gruesome manner. He once shot a snapping turtle so many times there was nothing left of it. When Leith took antidepressants prescribed by a psychiatrist, he became hyperactive and displayed bizarre behavior at school. He also began to exhibit chronic mood swings, depression, and lack of communication. He also exhibited suicidal tendencies and felt school officials were persecuting him. These aberrant behaviors culminated in the shooting.

When Joseph Piasecki first came to the school, he had developed a crisis plan. Before his murder, it had been used only twice. Now, ironically, it was going to be used in a crisis in which he was accused by a subordinate of being the antagonist. Leith was ultimately convicted of Piasecki's murder and was sentenced to life in prison.

Chelsea is a tight-knit community, and the school is its center. When students and teachers returned to school the day following the shooting, there were some 80 counselors and administrators from seven school districts to help restore normalcy. Nonetheless, the Chelsea school will probably never be the same.

The Standard Gravure Corporation: "Don't make me work the folder!"

On Saturday, September 14, 1989, 47-year-old Joseph T. Wesbecker returned to the Standard Gravure Corporation printing plant in Louisville, Kentucky. He was not there to work. He was there to seek retribution for perceived wrongs done him by various people in the company. According to newspaper accounts in *The Indianapolis Star,* Wesbecker had experienced a difficult life. His father died before he was one year old, and his mother treated him more like a brother than a son. The strongest figure in his life was his grandmother, who became his surrogate mother and seemed to have been his only stabilizing force. Even when Wesbecker worked at Fawcett Printing, his co-workers noticed some odd quirks about him. They nick-named him "Pinky": he was so obsessed with keeping clean that he constantly washed his hands—so often that they became discolored.

Wesbecker married and in the 1970s experienced some family problems. His oldest son developed scoliosis (curvature of the spine) and his youngest son had begun exposing himself in public. Wesbecker blamed both problems on a genetic imbalance that he felt he had passed on to his sons. He claimed his genetic code had been damaged by fumes from solvents used in the printing processes where he worked. In 1980, Wesbecker began treatment for depression with a psychiatrist, and in January of 1989, after being hospitalized repeatedly for mental illness, he was put on permanent psychiatric disability by the company.

Between 1980 and 1989, Wesbecker complained about

being forced to work "the folder," an important job that involved controlling an entire press run. It was a high-stress job that Wesbecker did not like. He repeatedly had asked to be removed from it. He complained that he hated the supervisor who made him work it. Wesbecker's psychiatrist wrote a letter to the company urging that he be removed from the folder.

During this period, Wesbecker made threats about different violent actions he might carry out against the company. At one point, he threatened to attach a bomb to a solvent-recovery system and blow the roof off the building. At times, he threatened to kill his superiors if they made him work the folder. At one point, it was reported, Wesbecker said, "Then me and old AK-AK will take care of it."

Wesbecker also had displayed signs of instability at home. He chopped up two lawnmowers with an ax and drove his car over them. In August, Wesbecker's grandmother died, leaving him without her stabilizing influence. He also learned that his disability pension was scheduled to be decreased in October, leaving his family with a reduced income. Three days before Wesbecker went back to Standard Gravure, his psychiatrist urged him to enter a psychiatric hospital.

The accounts of what happened early that Saturday morning are indeed gruesome. Wesbecker entered the plant armed with a loaded AK assault rifle in one hand and in the other a duffel bag filled with several handguns and thousands of rounds of ammunition purchased just weeks before the rampage. He rode an elevator to the company's third-floor executive offices. When the door opened, he opened fire. He killed one woman and critically injured a receptionist. He then strode down a hallway, looking into offices for people on his hit list but shooting almost anyone whom he came across. Within the short span of 20 minutes, Wesbecker had killed 7 employees and injured 13.

One of the injured recounted how "bodies flew through the air" as Wesbecker shot them. Wesbecker ended the carnage when he pulled a 9-mm pistol from his duffel bag, placed it under his chin, and pulled the trigger, making himself the eighth victim. One of the wounded later died in the hospital, making a total count of nine dead.

La Porte, Indiana: "Who's been at my desk?"

Harold Lang, sanitation employee of La Porte, Indiana, was sitting at a picnic table in a break room when the superintendent of the sanitation department came out of his office and asked the question that may have sparked the sequence of events that ended in violence: "Who's been in my desk?"

Lang reportedly replied, "The only one who has been in your desk is you." The superintendent took off his glasses and approached Lang, grabbed him, and pushed him down on the floor. Lang then grabbed the superintendent's hair, and they wrestled around. Lang was able to get up, took the superintendent's glasses, twisted them, and broke them saying, "This is what I'll do to you if you ever touch me again." The superintendent later apologized to Lang, saying he was sorry and that he was having a bad day.

Lang later called the mayor to tell him that he had a "psychotic" working for him and that the superintendent was "sick." The mayor told him that he was wrong and eventually hung up on him. Lang took sick leave the next day. On Friday of that week, he went to a hospital for "injuries." When asked how he had received the injuries, Lang replied they were caused by a murder attempt by his boss. The hospital asked Lang who would pay for treatment, and he said that the city would pay. The hospital called the mayor, who refused to pay for any treatment. When Lang called the superintendent, the superintendent reportedly said he couldn't pay because doing so would make him look bad. The superintendent again apologized.

When Lang tried to get fellow employees to intervene, they refused to be witnesses for him. Later, the superintendent called Lang's home to apologize once again. Lang's mother talked to the superintendent and even offered to replace his glasses as an act of good faith. The superintendent refused the offer.

Lang then sent a telegram to his congressman and the president of the United States to advise them of the situation in the sanitation department in La Porte, Indiana. He then took two weeks vacation. When he returned, he went to pick up his paycheck and was given a letter notifying him he was terminated, as he had previously requested. When he questioned this, he was told it was a confirmation of his notice of resignation verbally given to the superintendent shortly after the original incident.

When Lang's mother learned of the termination letter, she went to the mayor's home to talk to him about it. The mayor refused to talk to her because he had guests in the house at the time. Mrs. Lang, however, insisted upon talking then and reportedly refused to leave. The mayor virtually shoved the mother out of his house and closed the door.

A few weeks later, Lang taped a lawnmower muffler to the barrel of his handgun as a silencer, went to the mayor's home in the middle of the night, hid nearby waiting for the lights to go out, then entered through a kitchen window, went into the bedroom, and shot both the mayor and his wife. The wife died at the scene and the mayor died later from complications.

Although the murders did not happen in the workplace and therefore might not be classified as violence in the workplace, the actual sequence of events started in the workplace and involved co-workers.

Marion, Indiana: An Angry Spouse

Nina Leever was leaving the Thompson Consumer Electronics plant on September 1, 1994, after a 12-hour shift. She had worked at the plant for more than 20 years. Her husband, James, from whom she had filed for divorce about two months before, was waiting for her in the parking lot. Leever approached his soon-to-be ex-wife and, before anyone could intervene, shot her three times in the head and once in the groin with a .38-caliber handgun. Leaving Nina dead, he fled to his home in Alexandria, Indiana, where authorities later found him dead from a shot from the same gun.

According to the *Marion Chronicle-Tribune,* it was a tragic incident for the employees of Thompson. It left them quite shaken. Nina was well liked, and many employees felt there was something more they could have or should have done. They also wondered about their own future safety on the job. Although officials declared this to have been an isolated incident, it demonstrated the vulnerability of any employee at any time. Whether from an angry spouse or a disgruntled fellow employee, employers are required to protect employees at their place of work. Employers, therefore, must be alert to every situation that could spark violence.

U.S. Post Office: A Violent Place to Work?

Unfortunately, the U.S. Post Office has become infamous for the number of incidences of violence that have occurred at its various facilities. In Edmond, Oklahoma, a postal worker having problems both at home and at work killed 14 co-workers, wounded 6, and then took his own life.

In Ridgewood, New Jersey, a discharged postal worker killed his former supervisor and her male companion in the supervisor's home, and then went to his former workplace and killed two former co-workers there.

In 1991, at the Royal Oak, Michigan, post office, Thomas Paul McIlvane, a discharged employee, killed three former co-workers, wounded six, and shot himself. He and another of the wounded died later in the hospital. The U.S. House of Representatives Post Office and Civil Service Committee report on violence in the Postal Service indicated that union officials never reported numerous threats of violence made on the job by McIlvane. Postal officials acknowledged that the Postal Service had no established means by which employees could report threats made by co-workers.

In the Orange Glen Postal Substation in Escondido, California, a postal worker allegedly killed his wife at home, went to his workplace, killed two co-workers, and finally killed himself.

The Postal Service reported that between 1983 and 1989, 57% of work-related homicides in the Postal Service were committed by employees or former employees.

Meridian Mortgage Co.: "I'll show you big guys!"

In this incident, it was a *customer* who returned to a place where he had done business and vented his anger against the business owner.

One morning in February 1977, Tony Kiritsis, armed with a sawed-off shotgun, walked into the Meridian Mortgage Co. and took owner John Hall hostage. Kiritsis wired the barrel of the shotgun to the back of Hall's neck with a "deadman's rig," designed to cause the wire to pull the trigger of the gun should Kiritsis himself be shot by police. Any surprise move by the victim could also cause the trigger to be pulled. Kiritsis was demanding that Hall cancel his company's call for default on a mortgage the company held on property Kiritsis owned. He also demanded time on national television to explain to the nation why he had been forced to take Hall hostage. Kiritsis apparently wanted to make the event public to ensure that Hall could not renege on any promises he might make under duress. Most of all, he wanted this incident to send a message to everyone in the country. It appears that message in effect was, "Big guys, don't take advantage of us small guys. If you do, see what could happen to you!"

Kiritsis had purchased a piece of speculative commercial real estate that he mortgaged through Meridian Mortgage Co., which Hall owned. Kiritsis did not plan to hold the land vacant for long. He intended to find a buyer or a long-term tenant for whom to build. In either event, he would realize working capital and be able to proceed. However, such a buyer or tenant was not forthcoming, and he began to miss payments on the mortgage. Meridian Mortgage threatened foreclosure. Kiritsis was incensed because he claimed that Hall had discouraged all prospective clients Kiritsis had developed, hoping that Kiritsis would have to default on the loan.

After Kiritsis' television appearance, he surrendered and released Hall. He offered a "not guilty by reason of insanity" plea in court and was acquitted, but was required to submit to treatment in a mental hospital. He remained in the hospital for several years, never submitting to treatment or even examination before being released.

General Motors Acceptance Corporation: "Don't take my car away!"

Violence in the workplace does not always come from an employee, as evidenced in a shooting in the GMAC office in Jacksonville, Florida. A man carrying a gun, upset because the company had repossessed his car, walked into the office, slaughtered eight employees, wounded five, and then turned the .30-caliber semi-automatic weapon on himself.

Northwestern University: "You ruined my life!"

Professor Mario A. Ruggero, 51, was shot three times by a former lab assistant while walking through the parking lot of Northwestern University. John A. Costalupes, 45, had worked with the victim at the University of Minnesota *eight years* before, but it was reported that they never got along together. Costalupes accused Ruggero of cheating him out of credit for research Costalupes had helped with, the subject of a 1987 legal agreement between the two. As he approached Ruggero in the parking lot, Costalupes reportedly yelled, "You ruined my life," and opened fire. After shooting Ruggero, Costalupes returned to the University of Minnesota. He was attempting to get to the offices of Dean Shelley Chou when spotted by university personnel, who notified campus police. When police attempted to arrest Costalupes, he turned his gun on himself, committing suicide.

Ralston Food, Inc.: No Discernible Motive

In January 1995, employee Gerald Rieflin was charged with killing two co-workers and wounding two others when he walked into the packaging area of Ralston Food, Inc., in Cedar Rapids, Iowa, and began shooting. He left, went home, and held responding police at bay for two hours before surrendering. No motive had been determined at the time this case was reported in the media. Company officials shut down the factory after the shooting and called in crisis counselors to assist workers. Officials decided to suspend operations to permit a police investigation and "...to give employees time to come to terms with the situation," one official stated.

Workplace Violence: An American Phenomenon?

By all of these accounts, workplace violence is a fact and a phenomenon of modern American culture, one in need of immediate concern and affirmative action. In a 1993 survey by the Society for Human Resource Management, 67% of respondents reported some type of workplace violence in the past five years. Most of the violent acts were committed in offices, with plants being the next most vulnerable areas.

No organization can claim immunity. On April 25, 1994, *Time* magazine reported that workplace violence has occurred even in flower nurseries, pizza parlors, the cockpit of an airplane, and law offices.

It even happened in the FBI. On a hot August day in 1979, two FBI agents were in their El Centro, California, office doing paperwork when 30-year-old James Maloney arrived for an appointment to discuss his Freedom of Information request regarding a 1970 investigation into his suspected involvement with the Weatherman underground group. As Maloney entered the office, he immediately opened fire with a shotgun and, with two blasts, killed agents Charles Elmore and J. Robert Porter. He then put a .38 handgun into his own mouth and pulled the trigger.

Nearly half of workplace homicides in 1992 were in retail stores, primarily convenience stores, restaurants, drinking establishments, and auto service stations. Approximately 30 to 40% of workplace homicides are committed by an employee or former employee. The greatest majority of the remainder are random killings of employees and/or customers by criminals in the commission of a crime of greed. On the basis of a seven-day work week, an average of at least three employees are murdered on the job each day in the United States.

2

A TAXONOMY OF
WORKPLACE VIOLENCE

There may be no panacea for workplace violence. The good news is, however, that there are signs of potentially violent behavior that employers and co-workers can recognize and procedures both can take to reduce that potential.

There are three categories of perpetrators of workplace violence—employees, former employees, and nonemployees—and three types of situations, based upon the origin of the conflict and the location where it occurred. These three types of situations can be broken down into subtypes, depending upon whether the protagonists are employees, former or nonemployees vs. employees, or former or nonemployees vs. random victim(s).

Type 1: Violence Originates in the Workplace and Occurs in the Workplace

The first subtype is exemplified by the Chelsea, Michigan, and Standard Gravure Company incidents. A situation in the workplace develops, often as a result of a chain of events, to cause an employee to feel that he or she is a victim of unfair treatment. The employee then seeks to exact vengeance upon, or obtain retribution from, antagonist(s) and/or to make an example of them. Antagonists may be identified from among bosses, fellow employees, relatives, business owners, or others. Victims may even be people who just happen to be there when the incident occurs. In some cases, the victims are not specifically chosen by the perpetrator: anyone found in the establishment may satisfy by proxy either the retribution or vengeance needs of the perpetrator.

East Junior High School: "You ruined my career. Now you must pay!"

The second subtype is typified by a 1983 incident in Brentwood, New York, in which Robert O. Wickes, 34, invaded East Junior High School wearing army fatigues and carrying a .22-caliber rifle. Wickes walked into a social studies class just after noon and attempted to push the teacher out the door. The teacher called the school office and asked that the police be called. The principal came to the classroom, and Wickes immediately shot him in the face. He turned to the class and instructed the students to lift their faces up off their desks. Two weeks prior, after a physical altercation between Wickes and Louie Burgos, one of the students in the classroom, Wickes had been fired as a substitute teacher, and Burgos had been suspended. He identified Burgos from among the students and asked, "How long were you suspended?" Louie replied, "One week," and Wickes shot him.

Over the course of the next nine hours, students became sick or feigned illness, and Wickes let them go until only one of the students remained in the classroom. He issued an "epistle," saying in part, "I cried and no one heard. So now I cry on you, you dirty swine. You turned your back, so now I reciprocated, you see...power wins. Even so, I will paint the road with carnage...You kids messed up my career." At 10:05 p.m., the radio began playing "Fooling Yourself" by the Styx, a song about a "troubled young man" whose "head needs a rest." Wickes told authorities he was dedicating this song to his parents and brother. Just as the song came to its chorus, "Just take your best shot and don't blow it," Wickes put the gun to his own temple and pulled the trigger.

Every violent situation does not necessarily culminate in a shooting, but there always is some overt aggression, in the form of pushing, shoving, or fighting. In other instances, employees verbally attack each other or a supervisor who has disciplined or is disciplining them. When employees attack supervisors, it is often an attempt to intimidate them, to make them fearful of asserting their authority in the future.

Vengeance sometimes takes the form of destruction or damage to a fellow employee or manager's personal property, such as automobiles, clothing, and/or work equipment. Slashing the tires on a perceived antagonist's vehicle seems to be a common way for disgruntled employees to seek vengeance.

Kostoff-McKee Overhead Door Co.: The Second Time Around

The third subtype is exemplified by the case of Johnny Wayne Burns, who walked into this southeast-side Indianapolis business one January afternoon in 1995, fired a shot into the ceiling, and took all employees hostage. He subsequently released everyone except Sheree Hughes. After 5 1/2 hours, he came out with Hughes and shot himself in the stomach with his .22-caliber gun before surrendering to the sheriff. What made this incident particularly unusual is that this was the second time around for both!

In the earlier incident, Burns, a former employee, entered the company at about 1:00 p.m. on a hot August afternoon in 1989 and, at gunpoint, took Hughes hostage. About an hour later, he released her unharmed.

His motive in either instance was not determined. Burns already had served two years in prison on a 1984 conviction for the murder of Shellie Adams, 24, following a dispute.

Type 2: Violence Originates in the Workplace but Occurs Outside the Workplace

This type is exemplified by the La Porte city worker. That situation originated in the workplace but ultimately culminated in the death of the mayor and his wife in their home. An employee who perceived himself to be a victim of unjust treatment in the workplace was the perpetrator in that event. The employee first sought some kind of retribution and then, thwarted in this effort, it appears his intent evolved into one of sheer vengeance.

Of course, all such situations do not end in murder. On another occasion, after being disciplined by a supervisor, an employee sought retribution by destroying the mailbox at the supervisor's home. Destruction of property is a mode of intimidation; at the same time, it bolsters the perpetrator's sense of power to avoid being a "victim."

Type 3: Violence Originates Outside the Workplace and Occurs in the Workplace

Such was the situation that occurred at the Thompson Consumer Electronics plant in Marion, Indiana. The employee was having difficulty with her spouse at home, which ended with her being shot at her workplace.

In the case of Meridian Mortgage Co., it is not known

if Kiritsis' accusations against the company were true. If so, then the incident would fit into Type 1. If the accusations were unfounded (based upon his defense of insanity, that is a possibility), it would fit into Type 3.

The greatest number of incidents of violence in the workplace occur as a result of attempted robberies by nonemployees, primarily in retail fast-food stores, restaurants, convenience stores, and service stations. This category accounts for approximately half of all homicides in the workplace each year.

A different type of violence that originates outside the workplace, but manifests inside the workplace, has been typified by terrorist attacks on specific organizations and/or robberies wherein physical violence has occurred. Although these violent acts occurred in workplaces, they usually were motivated by political reasons or by the need for money to finance the terrorists' causes. The organization was either a symbol of protest, providing a stage for widespread publicity of the event, or a financial institution, chosen with robbery or extortion as the motive. A good example of this type of workplace violence is the bombing of the World Trade Towers in New York City, allegedly by foreign Muslim extremists. Regardless of the type of violence that victims suffer, all types have similar effects on workers: fear, anxiety, apprehension, dissension, distraction, and disruption of production.

The Cost of Workplace Violence

Data on the cost of workplace violence are incomplete, but one survey by the Northwestern National Life Insurance Company indicated that in 1993, 2.2 million workers in U.S. workplaces were physically attacked, 6.3 million were threatened, and 16.1 million were harassed. The 1992 National Crime Victimization Survey reported

667,978 cases of violence in the workplaces of America that year. There are estimates that these incidents cost employers $4.2 billion. In the absence of a formal reporting system, complete and accurate statistics upon which to estimate total primary and secondary costs to employers and victims in an average year are nonexistent.

The secondary effects are very difficult to identify, let alone quantify in dollars. There are direct and indirect costs to the employer, primary and secondary costs to employees and their families, and primary and secondary costs to nonemployee victims and their families.

Costs to the Organization

Primary Costs

- **Medical costs** (physical and psychological)—Employees and third-party victims who claim reimbursement for injuries, psychological counseling, and funeral costs
- **Lost productivity**—Downtime during the event and after the event, lost productivity from employees during the event or until those who do not return are replaced, and nonproductivity during the time required to repair or replace equipment
- **Property damage**—Facilities and equipment destroyed or damaged and the cost of lost or damaged private property of victims
- **Lost sales**—Lost sales during the event, due both to downtime for cleanup and repairs and to sales lost because customers are fearful of visiting the premises
- **Legal fees**—Defense of suits of victims and any adverse judgments against the company

Secondary Costs

- **Medical costs** (physical and psychological)—Medical costs for employees not directly involved but suffering effects directly attributable to the event

- **Lost productivity**—Decrease in the productivity of victims and co-workers due to residual fear, anger, or resentment between participants, among their followers, or on the part of witnesses, which can damage the integrity and efficiency of operations well into the future
- **Preventive measures**—New procedures and/or additional security personnel/equipment that may be needed in order to inhibit or prevent similar occurrences in the future

3

CAUSES OF WORKPLACE VIOLENCE

Obviously, there are a variety of causes of violence in the workplace. The previously cited Society for Human Resource Management study found that approximately 38% of all workplace violence was caused by personality conflicts and related stress.

Threat to Job

Among stresses leading to workplace violence are the pressures of losing, or the fear of losing, one's job. Such fear is common today in the midst of "downsizing" and "rightsizing": the trimming of personnel in organizations due to re-engineering or acquisitions and mergers. The effects are particularly traumatic because there are often no previous warnings that could have allowed an employee to prepare for or prevent the loss of the job.

Poor work performance or violation of company rules and policies often result in job loss, or the threat of it. Income and job security are basic security needs—the bottom level of psychologist Abraham Maslow's Hierarchy of Needs. When an employee's attention is focused on

satisfying these basic survival needs, all other considerations become secondary.

According to need theory, people who have been properly civilized within their native culture will attempt to
satisfy their needs legally, morally, and realistically. However, if sufficient barriers exist to inhibit or prevent satisfaction of basic needs, some people will resort to illegal,
immoral, and/or unrealistic means to satisfy these needs.
When the job and the income that provide the means to
meet needs are threatened, and if the barriers cannot be
removed legally, morally, or realistically, some people seek
to remove these barriers in other, less acceptable ways or
means. Even the most psychologically balanced persons
have a point at which, after all positive options have
failed, they will attack to destroy those barriers, or at
least "alter" them. The criticality point is the level of coping skill and the inventory of alternative behaviors one
possesses, or the level one perceives one possesses. If the
employee perceives that the loss of a job is handled unfairly by management and that there is no other recourse,
the employee may choose to act out of frustrated desperation and anger.

Threat to Person

Many organizations have autocratic, centralized power
structures that delegate very little power to subordinates
at any level, particularly to production employees. Such
a system breeds arbitrary behavior on the part of management and frustration and resentment among employees. If an employee is arbitrarily fired or threatened with
job loss, or even criticized or disciplined unfairly, this
person perceives no way to respond to maintain dignity.
Such a frustration, particularly if there has been a history of such events, is sufficient to prompt some people
to resort to overt, violent reactions.

In nearly every instance of employee or ex-employee violence studied by the authors, the event was preceded by an event or series of events in which the employee suffered negative consequences due to what was perceived as unfair and prejudicial behavior by superiors.

An employee who works in an organization that has a centralized, authoritative managerial structure has a perception that employees are told what to do, when to do it, and how to do it, with no input of their own into the job. In this work environment, people tend to suffer a loss of self-esteem. An employee may compare the actions of the supervisor/manager to those of a dictator. The worker may also believe that work problems cannot be solved because of bureaucracy and the impersonal, uncaring nature of the organization and its leaders.

Since this worker feels like a victim of circumstance and cannot identify any internal resources for either positively reacting to or changing the circumstance, the person tends to attack to respond aggressively to the perceived threat. Insensitive bosses are identified as antagonists, as they well may be, and the ultimate response of the employee is to attack to remove or destroy these antagonists.

When this circumstance begins to evolve, the employee usually attempts to rally co-workers to help out, involving them in a concerted move against a certain supervisor or management in general. Most often, the other workers do not wish to become personally involved in the matter and fail to support the employee. This is viewed as failed allegiance. "If the other workers are not on my side," the employee reasons, "by definition, they are against me." The employee is soon unable to differentiate between the primary antagonist(s) and the "turncoat" co-workers.

This inability to solve personal problems, or even to get someone in the organization to listen, evokes a perceived state of powerlessness. In an attempt to regain that power, or to get rid of the person(s) who took that power away, the employee may become very focused, mission-oriented, and self-righteous. At that point, it may become very difficult to reach this person with logic or reason.

By the account of the wife of the Chelsea teacher, it was obvious he was determined to kill the superintendent. He was so focused on this mission that there was no one, including his wife, who could stop him. He was willing to sacrifice himself in the service of his mission, in order to see his righteous sense of justice prevail.

Extended Working Hours

Long work hours overburden some employees by increasing demands while diminishing the time to achieve them. Extended work hours also reduce rest, recreation, and exercise times that are important in both reducing stress and increasing physical and mental resistance to stress. When one feels overwhelmed, one begins to feel a sense of helplessness—that it is impossible to get out from under all of one's burdens. Persistent stress causes anxiety and a reduced ability to interpret either the nature of situations or the appropriate and effective responses to them. Undoubtedly, this affects fellow employees who must interact with the troubled person. They are not likely to understand the person's behavior, only recognizing that it is not functional and that the person is neither pleasant nor cooperative. Over a period of time, fellow employees may begin to ostracize the employee, whom they see as the problem, just as the human body deals with a foreign object, such as a splinter in a finger.

However, as in the finger, the problem gets worse before it gets better. If left unattended, the finger eventually forces out the foreign object and only then begins to heal. If the effects of longer hours overburden an employee over a significant period of time, undoubtedly the person's ability to function will be impaired. Whether or not the employee finally loses control will depend upon several other internal and external factors, but, suffice to say, this person is a candidate for potentially violent behavior.

Personality Conflicts

Interpersonal conflicts amongst and between workers and managers are probably the most frequent and apparent causes of violence. "Apparent" is emphasized because often there are significant personal factors disputants have brought with them to work, and the conflicts are a result of those underlying problems. In such an event, the conflicts at work are more difficult to resolve. The work disputes, in many instances, are a convenient means of displacing or projecting these underlying frustrations. Disputes at work, then, simply become the straws that break the camel's back.

Of course, there are instances of legitimate personality conflict. No matter how much anyone would like to deny it, there are some people who just rub others the wrong way. It can happen between peers, supervisors, or subordinates. Too often, none of them have the necessary skills to positively manage interpersonal conflict. The situation proceeds then to develop into a negative cause-and-effect spiral that can ultimately become violent.

The Paper Fight

A General Motors supervisor reported a fight in a GM plant involving a newspaper. One employee had purchased a newspaper, and another employee was reading it. The first employee, a female, grabbed the paper in an attempt to take it away from the other employee, a male. In the ensuing struggle, the female was thrown into a nearby set of lockers, and her arm was broken. But that was not the end of it. The woman's husband was also an employee at the same plant. When he heard what had happened to his wife, he came to the other man's work area and physically attacked him. In that struggle, the paper reader's ankle was broken.

In this instance, the supervisor found the events amusing, apparently ignoring the costs, effects, and implications of the matter. Amusing or not, it was fortunate this situation did not result in more than just broken bones.

Domestic Turbulence

On February 28, 1994, Julian B. Trammel set a car on fire and drove it into the outside wall of the offices of a Gloucester, Virginia, law firm that was representing his wife in her divorce proceedings against him. Trammel then entered the law office through the back door and began shooting. As Trammel exited the building, a Virginia state trooper confronted Trammel and shot and killed him. Mrs. Trammel was filing for divorce because of her husband's "violent and threatening behavior as well as physical abuse."

Personality/Character Disorders

"Character" can be defined as one's set of values and the degree of self-government one commands to adhere to that value system. If one's character incorporates values such as responsibility, unselfishness, sensitivity to others, cooperation, and a win–win attitude toward controversy, and one is able to live by these values, this person is more likely to become a model employee and co-worker. On the contrary, if the character is devoid of these values, there is no foundation by which to guide and discipline oneself, allowing the individual to become unpredictable and untrustworthy.

"Personality" is one's unique set of behavioral traits, including manners of expression and ways of interacting with others. As one's personality develops through early childhood and adolescence, it becomes more and more patterned and predictable. Personality is both complex and complicated. It embodies one's self-concept and self-esteem (the degree to which a person believes that he or she is worthwhile and deserving). Although there are some normal personalities that are more interpersonally functional than others, there are others which are abnormal, or "disordered."

Although personality is affected by both heredity and environment, personality disorders are, by definition, learning disorders. People have failed to learn appropriate and effective behavioral responses to some or several typical life frustrations. Some of these disorders result in a personality having an unrealistic perception of "rights" and "responsibilities," resulting in demands that their needs and preferences be satisfied before those of others. These personalities are insensitive to the rights and privileges of others, and such people tend to be bossy, domineering, threatening, and even violent if they feel their own rights are threatened. They whine, complain, and feel anger and resentment when they do not get their way. In some cases, they never developed sufficient control to govern their tempers. Even in moments of frustration that other people might simply shrug off, they unexpectedly strike out verbally or physically. To themselves, their own behavioral modes are "normal," not understanding how others could perceive them as unreasonable or unacceptable.

There are four basic personality dimensions:

1. **Extroversion vs. introversion**—This dimension ranges from the sociable, talkative, and assertive to the retiring, sober, reserved, and cautious.
2. **Agreeableness**—This spectrum encompasses the good-natured, gentle, and cooperative to the irritable, ruthless, and inflexible.

3. **Conscientiousness**—This ranges from careful, thorough, responsible and self-disciplined to irresponsible, disorganized, and unscrupulous.
4. **Emotional stability**—On one end, this type is calm, enthusiastic, and secure. On the other, this type is anxious, depressed, emotional, excitable, and insecure.

Personality also affects how one interprets the events that occur in life. Interpersonal relationships are a central part of a person's life. Relatives, friends, lovers, supervisors, subordinates, and co-workers normally have a significant influence on a person's perceptions, since they share the social values and interpretive biases of their common culture. If one willingly segregates oneself from normal personal bonds and social interactions, the person becomes divorced as well from the mainstream values and beliefs. The extent of this isolation from these cultures determines the degree to which the person thinks and acts on the basis of singularly personal logical constructs. Often, resultant behaviors either are disconsonant with the mainstream cultures or simply are inappropriate or ineffective.

Research Regarding Personality, Mental Health, and Behavior

According to the E. Megargee model of predicting violence, three personality factors need to be assessed:

- **Motivation**—In the assessment of violence, two types of aggression must be considered:
  1. *Angry aggression*—This type of aggression is motivated by a desire to harm someone and is reinforced by the victim's pain and suffering.
  2. *Instrumental aggression*—This type of aggression is a means to some other end and has other rein-

forcements (for example, shooting a person in the commission of a robbery).

- **Inhibition**—Internal inhibitions are personal taboos against engaging in violent behavior or any other act that conflicts with internalized values. If inhibitions exceed motivation, the person refrains from prohibited behavior. However, inhibitions can be weakened by alcohol or other psychoactive substances.
- **Habit**—Habits are behavioral "patterns"; that is, they are programmed responses to typical stimuli. They are formed on the basis of perceived positive reinforcement of past behaviors. The more violent acts committed in the past that were perceived as having been rewarded instead of punished, the more likely it is that they will be repeated in the future. This pattern of violent behavior develops into habit, and that habit may prevail over any logical inhibitions against violence.

Sigmund Freud first developed personality theory in the context of mental health, describing two basic needs common to every person:

1. **The need for love**—An intimate relationship with another person or family unit
2. **The need for work**—A purposeful activity that will identify the person's role in and contribution to society

Gordon Allport expanded Freud's list by adding the following criteria for sound mental health:

1. A unifying philosophy that gives purpose to one's life
2. Self-extension to such meaningful spheres of human endeavor as one's marital partner and one's work
3. The capacity for loving relationships free of crippling possessiveness and jealousy
4. Emotional security and self-acceptance
5. Accurate self-insight

Clayton Alderfer, in his Existence/Relatedness/Growth (ERG) Theory of Needs, asserted that there are three groups of core needs, as follows:

1. **Existence**—This group of needs is concerned with providing one's basic requirements for material existence, such as physiological and safety needs. This need is satisfied by money earned in a job to buy food, home, clothing, etc.
2. **Relatedness**—This group of needs centers on or is built upon the desire to establish and maintain interpersonal relationships. Since one usually spends approximately half of one's waking hours on the job, this need is normally satisfied at least to some degree by one's co-workers.
3. **Growth**—These needs are met by one's personal development. Obviously, one's job, career, or profession provides for significant satisfaction of growth needs.

Alderfer's ERG theory further claims that more than one need may be influential at the same time. If the gratification of a higher-level need is frustrated, the desire to satisfy a lower-level need will increase. Alderfer identifies this phenomenon as the "frustration–aggression dimension." Its relevance on the job is that even when the upper-level needs are frustrated, the job still provides for the basic physiological needs upon which one would then be focused. If, at that point, something happens to threaten the job, the person's basic needs are significantly threatened. If there are not mitigating factors to relieve the pressure, the person may become desperate and panicky.

In 1939, psychologist John Dollard explained that when frustration occurs, it produces some form of aggression, and that in fact aggression never occurs *except* as a result of frustration. The term "frustration" simply means the psychophysiological effect of having one's needs blocked. If frustration is significant and persistent over a long period of time and there appears to be no hope of relief, one may well perceive that one's existence is being threatened.

If one cannot detour barriers, one may resort to removing them. If one's work is a major contributor to need satisfaction, as the above authorities suggest it is for most people, and if the job is lost, this alone is enough to provoke some people to illogical, desperate behavior. However, when aspects of the job itself become the actual barriers, such as antagonisms with co-workers or bosses, the frustrations are intensified and the potential for violence increased.

Organizations must be alert and sensitive to the psychological well-being of their employees, attempt to maximize the potential for need satisfaction, minimize the potential for frustration, and watch for behaviors consistent with the typologies of workplace violence.

Mental Illness

In December 1993, Alan Winterbourne, an unemployed computer engineer, entered the Oxnard, California, unemployment office and began shooting, killing three people. Upon leaving that office, he was confronted by a police officer, whom he killed. He wounded three other people on his way to another unemployment office in Ventura, where he was confronted again by police. This time, he was killed. Winterbourne had a history of mental instability and involvement in disputes with governmental agencies. A former co-worker reported that Winterbourne had behaved so irrationally that he had complained to their boss that Winterbourne "might come in and shoot me."

The genesis of mental illness is still being argued by the experts. Some say it is inherited, others claim it is caused by environmental influences, and still others insist it is a result of chemical imbalances in the body. Mental illness is probably rooted in all of these theories. Whatever the cause, mental illness is common, and many of the afflicted are left to function on their own in society with little or no help. Those who are in the workplace are left to compete without the full capabilities to do so.

In the late 1960s, there was a reversal in thinking regarding the manner of care of America's mentally ill: the mentally ill were "de-institutionalized," put back into society to be treated on an out-patient basis, with the following results:

- In 1968, there were almost 400,000 psychiatric in-patients in U.S. mental institutions. Today, in 1996, there are just over 100,000.
- In 1969, the average in-patient term for psychiatric patients was 421 days. Today it is less than 175 days.
- Since 1975, incidents involving the mentally ill that required police services have increased by more than 200% in most major cities.
- In 1955, 75% of the mentally ill were treated as in-patients. By 1985, 75% of their treatment was on an out-patient basis.

Most of those who were de-institutionalized 30 years ago are still ill, but they are now in the mainstream of society. That is, they are attempting to live normal lives in a very competitive nation, and many of them are in the workplace trying to make a living. The big difference is that many lack coping skills. Interpersonal problems in the workplace commonly cause strained relationships, lack of full cooperation, inefficiency, and aggravation. However, as with Joseph Wesbecker at the Standard Gravure Co. and Robert Wickes at East Junior High School, mentioned in Chapter 1, people who are unable to perceive or interpret reality have difficulty forming appropriate and effective responses to perceived problems that developed in their workplaces. Frustrated, they struck out to destroy their perceived antagonists.

In the Lang case in La Porte and the Kiritsis case in Indianapolis, also discussed in Chapter 1, each appeared to most of his co-workers or acquaintances to be eccentric but otherwise normal. In the Wesbecker and Wickes cases, each was psychotic—they had lost contact with reality. Even though Kiritsis was found not guilty by reason of insanity, it is doubtful that either he or Lang was psychotic. Both Lang and Kiritsis, it would appear, were mentally unstable at the time of their respective violent events, and probably had been for a significant time. It would appear from each of their backgrounds that neither had developed functional skills sufficient to effectively deal with people. Lacking such skills, both had difficulty forming positive responses in disputes. Consequently, they suffered a perceived loss of power and control, viewing themselves as victims when unable to compete or to effectively engage others in controversy. Such experiences made them generally apprehensive of others' motives, fearful they might be taken advantage of. Such apprehensions usually were unfounded, and the subjects of those suspicions naturally resented such attitudes, further straining relationships. The result was a negative cause-and-effect spiral that left them suspicious of nearly everyone they knew, leaving them virtually no one to trust.

An attitude of distrust and a defensive temperament do not bode well for work relationships in which naturally suspicious people share approximately one half of their waking hours with other people. Even in seemingly normal situations, there may be an underlying negative current, and all it takes is the proverbial spark to propel these persons into a violent response.

Lack of Dispute-Resolution Skills

One need not be mentally ill or unstable to aggravate relationships or resort to violence. All people have a point at which they lose their tempers. Even the most pacific or meek will fight back at some point. There are proven techniques and processes of positive dispute resolution, but too few people possess them.

In America, our heritage is the independent frontiers-man—killing or being killed, winning or losing. Our capitalistic economic system favors the innovative, tough entrepreneur who forges an idea into an industry, beating his competitors or, better yet, forcing them right out of business. Our culture has idealized the win–lose tactic in all interactions.

The urban riots of the 1960s were the first popular introduction of the win–win approach to dispute resolution. When parties in dispute adopt a win–lose attitude, or are ignorant of the alternative, all parties are destined to lose, albeit sometimes one more than the other(s). Conversely, a win–win approach sometimes results in one party winning more than the other(s), but at least both win instead of both losing.

Since conflict is normal, its occurrence in the workplace is normal. Conflict provides the opportunity for problems to be identified in order that they may be eliminated. Since there are too few employees who know how to positively manage disputes, problems are more often intensified instead of resolved, sometimes erupting into violence.

General Life Stress

All workplace violence is not generated in the workplace, however. There are innumerable other circumstances that create increasing amounts of stress on people, at home, in extended familial relationships, and in other social institutions, even churches or synagogues. A divorce, or an impending one, generates an enormous amount of stress, as exemplified by the incident at the Marion, Indiana, plant.

The death of a family member or friend obviously has a significant impact. In the Joseph Wesbecker case, the "last straw" may have been the death of his grandmother.

Substance Abuse

The introduction of chemical substances into the body and mind has a devastating effect upon one's perceptions and thought processes. Thinking, moods, and behavior are rendered unpredictable. The record is clear that alcohol or drugs play a major role in workplace violence. Many perpetrators have had a dependency on drugs or alcohol, and many drug-dependent or alcoholic employees are in the workplace today.

Chemical abuses include antidepressants, speed, cocaine, heroin, and marijuana, among myriad others. The postal employee in the Orange Glen station was suspected of abusing alcohol, which has historically been responsible for most of the violent behavior in the workplace. There have been instances of metabolic and mental disturbances and violent behaviors in users of anabolic steroids, particularly during withdrawal after periods of heavy use.

Prescription drugs sometimes have deleterious side effects, particularly if taken improperly or mixed with other drugs, which can produce unexpected side effects. The teacher in Chelsea and the printing plant employee in Louisville had been taking prescription drugs for depression prior to their violent outbursts.

Even caffeine—found in coffee, most carbonated beverages, and chocolate—is suspected of causing headaches and influencing mood.

Professor John J. Prince, of Central Missouri State University, reports that certain chemical solvents commonly found in some work environments can cause psychological changes in workers who are exposed to them, resulting in erratic or violent behavior. He indicates that these solvents can penetrate into the bloodstream by inhalation or absorption through the skin. The symptoms, which are similar to those of drug abuse, include hallucinations, feelings of great strength and invulner-

ability, and lowered inhibitions. The problem is complicated by the insidious nature of the attacks, making it
difficult for workers, co-workers, or management to realize what is causing the aberrant behaviors.

Many organizations today are implementing fitness
programs to advise and counsel employees on eating,
exercise, and stress management. Most larger organizations have employee assistance plans to aid employees
who develop problems in any of these areas. The benefits
include lower absenteeism, increased productivity, fewer
health insurance claims, and greater harmony in employee relationships.

Violence as a Cultural Norm

H. Rap Brown, 1960s civil rights radical activist, once
observed, "Violence is as American as cherry pie." Brown
himself died unexpectedly when a bomb he was trans-
porting in an auto accidently detonated under his feet.

In the United States each year more than 50,000
people are murdered or commit suicide. The family is the
greatest generator of the violence that often spills over
into the workplace.

- **Spouse abuse**—This is a problem that continues to
  grow. Although there are some reports of men being
  abused by their wives, the data indicate that women
  are more likely to be abused by men.
- **Child abuse**—This is sometimes a catch-all term used
  to refer to nonaccidental physical attacks on or injury
  to children by individuals caring for them.
- **Parent abuse**—This is abuse to one or more of a child's
  elderly parents.

Statistics indicate that all forms of family violence are on
the rise in the United States—the harbinger of a greater
incidence of violence in the workplace.

There are congressional committees, citizens' groups, and scholars doing research on how prominent and provocative violence is interwoven into the fabric of our culture. Some cite the fact that the United States has one of the highest homicide rates among civilized nations. They point to the number of violent acts depicted on television each week, claiming that it actively and/or passively influences its viewers, often young viewers. The movie industry, which preceded television, produced the same diet of violence for its audiences, from cowboys and Indians, cops and robbers, and family violence to world wars. Even if the constant exposure to violence does not commonly incite people to commit it, critics claim that it inures them to the phenomenon, rendering them insensitive to the effects of its realities in life.

The more accusative critics claim the constant diet of violence legitimizes its use in the minds of those who, in their upbringing, were never introduced to other, more positive, behavioral responses. As previously discussed, "habits," according to social learning theorists, are formed on the basis of which behaviors historically were perceived as positively reinforced. Current violent behavior, then, is a result of past experience. Learning the habit of reacting with violence proceeds in the same manner as does learning of all other habits. Very simply, if one lives with violence at home, as observer or victim, or witnesses violence in school, in the streets, on television, in the theaters, and in many other social arenas, then one may well learn that the use of violence to solve problems is "normal." Being "normal" is perceived by some as a *de facto* positive reinforcement. When violent response to frustration becomes one's habit and when frustration has built up over time from several areas of one's life, it takes only a minor incident to trigger that violence.

4

PROFILES VS. BEHAVIORAL TYPOLOGIES

Profiles

Although some expert sources have offered a profile of the violent employee, it may be misleading to attempt to create one. Such a definitive profile might be too exclusive and therefore dangerously misleading, even disarming. A description of a "typical" violent employee is merely the description of the composite average of a random group of people known to have committed violent acts in the workplace. In the late 1940s, an attempt was made to create the "ideal woman" by using the best of body features from among Hollywood's prettiest female stars. The resulting figure was disproportionate and ugly, not typifying at all what had been intended. Virtually no one who would act out violently in the workplace would possess *all* of the characteristics of a profile. On the other hand, someone who happened to possess all of the profile characteristics might possess enough self-control not to behave violently. The fact that someone fits the profile might even cause fellow employees to treat the worker in an alienating manner, possibly provoking a self-fulfilling prophecy. Such false fears could cause a negative reaction in the workplace, creating a problem where previously there had been none. Such are the dangers of a "profile." At the same time, however, to ignore the behavioral typologies of potentially violent people could be a serious, even fatal, oversight.

Behavioral "Typologies" of Violent People

There are no characteristics common to *all* violent people. However, there are certain traits and behaviors that are typical among people who become violent. Organizations should make employees aware of these and encourage vigilance in recognizing their occurrence among subordinates or co-workers in order that preventive measures might be initiated.

White males between 30 and 50 years of age have been the most prominent perpetrators of significant violence in the workplace. Women do not seem to be as prone to interpersonally violent behavior as are men. There are documented cases of violence by females, however, such as the disgruntled female employee at the Eveready Battery Company in Bennington, Vermont, who shot and killed the plant manager and wounded two other workers with a 9-mm pistol.

Since the greatest number of violent incidents have been by males, the following typologies will typify males. There are three categories:

1. Asocial
2. Dyssocial
3. Mental

Asocial

By definition, this type is generally uncomfortable around other people, preferring to live and work in the absence of other people, except for family members. He lacks interpersonal and social skills, is quiet, and internalizes interpersonal conflict and frustrations. When frustrations build over a period of time, it takes only a minor incident to finally overwhelm him, and he "explodes."

Other people within his life circle probably would describe him as a person who keeps to himself, an introvert. He is not well known by neighbors or co-workers with whom he shares a close physical proximity. He chooses to remain distant from others, who may perceive him as being "aloof." By being withdrawn, he becomes isolated. After awhile, he develops his own values and habits which may be quite different from those of the majority, rendering him a little "odd" or eccentric in their eyes.

Outside Stress

The Asocial is affected by stressors outside the job as well as those in the job, all of which combine to overwhelm him. Outside stressors come from all dimensions within one's life circle, but most often they emanate from within the immediate family. These problems may have been chronic, and he perceives them as "unsolvable." If he is going through a divorce, he sees himself as the blameless victim and his spouse as unreasonable and unfair. He expects some degree of sympathy from others, and if it is not forthcoming, he believes they are "on her side" and therefore against him.

Marital or financial problems are common, but most people's current coping problems originated in their own rearing family. If parents and siblings are still within his life circle, they more than likely still contribute to his psychological baggage.

Hypersensitivity

He is extremely sensitive to criticism from all sources. Supervisors and co-workers can hurt his feelings without even knowing it. Since he tends not to respond overtly to resolve or expel problems, he retains the hurt internally. Resentment builds with each succeeding incident. This scenario is particularly aggravated if the incident was criticism from a supervisor and involved only a minor act of discipline.

Inability to Accept Blame

This person has a tendency to reject not only criticism but also any responsibility or culpability for negative behavior. When either the supervisor or a co-worker attempts to discuss an error in a positive, coaching approach, he perceives it as an attempt to "blame" him. He rejects fault or blame and attempts to displace it on co-workers or projects it back upon the supervisor, the organization, or "society." He views any attempt to help him learn from the past as unnecessary and unfairly focused upon his faults.

Often he appears resentful of authority. He is not naturally hostile to authority, but because he is so easily alienated, he becomes resentful and resistant. This happens first on a personal basis and often grows into a general feeling of unfair treatment by others, even "persecution."

He has an unrealistic concept of justice. He believes that others receive too little punishment for their transgressions, whereas he feels himself to be chastised when he wasn't even wrong. Robert Wickes, the Brentwood, New York, school teacher described in Chapter 2, was a very explicit example of this mindset.

Rigidity

The Asocial type does not possess a wide range of coping skills. He fears and avoids new challenges for fear of mistakes, failure, or criticism. Therefore, he resists assuming new or additional responsibilities on the job. He is quick to define "boundaries" of authority and responsibility, guarding his territory and resisting being asked to "help out" with what he sees as "someone else's work." This rigidity governs all other activities and interests in life, including those that he feels he can control.

Since control is a prominent focus in his life, he tends to "overcontrol." For those activities that he considers important and for which he accepts responsibility, he makes extreme effort to ensure they are done "right." He avoids the negative and accrues the positive by garnering approval through achievement. Many normal people are guided by this simple theorem, but the Asocial depends upon it.

Secrecy

He tends to avoid interpersonal conversation, but when he does engage in it, he hides behind a superficial "service personality," revealing very little about his true personal life. What little conversation he may have is irrelevant small talk, complaints about his disadvantages in life or mistreatment by others. He prefers to focus on the problems of the past or unrealistic plans and hopes for the future. Seldom does he focus on realistic behaviors to cope with the present.

Neither co-workers nor supervisors ever really get to know him very well. He takes virtually no one into his confidence. Consequently, the caring and sharing relationships that can evolve among co-workers seldom develop with him. Neither does allegiance to co-workers, workgroups, or the employer. Therefore, he has fewer internal counterforces inhibiting his overt alienation of others.

Possessiveness

His personal privacy, few relationships in life, material possessions, and sometimes even his job are fiercely guarded as the few things that mean anything to him. A threat to any of these elicits a hostile, protective response much greater than others would deem necessary. Arguments with co-workers over such minor things as picking up his newspaper to read on a break without his permission can provoke unreasonably protective responses. He is territorial in defining what physical space (such as workstation, desk, equipment, etc.), possessions, responsibility, and authority are his. Anything that interrupts or disturbs his routine or depreciates his sense of protective control over what he believes he owns irritates and threatens him. He can be expected at some point to act out in desperate ways to re-establish routine and control.

Focus on Work

If his job is highly valued, it is because the job has become an important part of his life and a rare source of individual identification and pride. It is "his" job, and he feels his unique skill and expertise are deserving of people's respect. He derives a sense of identity, prestige, purpose, and power from his job and whatever affiliation he requires.

During people's most vital years, many tend to focus strongly on their work. Most of the time during these years is spent working, thinking about work, or traveling to and from work. When people feel good about work, they tend to feel good about themselves. When they feel that their work is unsatisfying or unrewarding, they no longer feel good about themselves or about anything or anyone else. Work can provide order in people's lives—a reason to get up in the morning, a specific somewhere to go. Work also provides the guideline by which some people measure success and failure.

Should difficulties arise with co-workers or management that would threaten the job of the Asocial, it would be considered a major personal threat. He might even equate an internal move within the organization with losing his job. A threat to the job often provokes him to overreact to protect it. Since his coping skills are limited, those protective acts may be provocative acts, serving only to aggravate the circumstance and trigger a negative cause-and-effect spiral.

Power Dependence

Since he overvalues power and control in all aspects of his life, he depends upon symbols of power. Position and authority may be legitimate sources of power, and he certainly seeks them. But he may have to depend on other sources, such as collecting or owning guns or other weapons or belonging to organizations such as the National Guard, which he also considers potent symbols of power.

A good example of this love of power was Joseph Wesbecker's comment in the Standard Gravure Co. case, cited in Chapter 1: "Me and old AK-AK will take care of it." Wesbecker had legally acquired all of his ammunition just weeks before the shootings. The teacher in the Chelsea case, also in Chapter 1, was a gun collector. The discharged worker at the Elgar Company in California had a large gun collection and spent a great amount of time at target practice. Most of his weapons, as is often the case, were acquired legally. In the Edmond, Oklahoma, post office case, the assailant was a member of the Oklahoma National Guard, was a weapons instructor and member of the marksmanship team, and, as such, was allowed to check out all of the weapons and ammunition he wanted at any time.

Violent Past

This person has typically had problems coping throughout his life, and when stresses have become intolerable, he has reacted in violent frustration. Most likely, the events have been within family, the neighborhood, or, if he is old enough, past work environments. If there is any one "best" predictor of future violence, it is past violence.

The postal worker in Royal Oak, Michigan, had a series of problems with co-workers and other people. He had once been suspended for fighting with customers on his postal route. He was known to have a short fuse. Johnny W. Burns, in the Kostoff-McKee Overhead Door Co. case in Chapter 2, had been convicted in the death of a girlfriend and had invaded a former employer's premises twice in the past ten years, taking a hostage each time.

Fatalism

The Asocial person feels that what happens to him in life is a function of external conditions, circumstances, and luck, whether good or bad. He believes that his fate is more in the hands of others than in his own. He blames bad luck or unfair treatment by others for his condition in life.

Dyssocial

The Dyssocial type is much more spontaneous and outwardly aggressive than the Asocial. He holds nothing back when angry and, as he is easily angered, strikes out often. He has a learned resentment of any authority, because he perceives that it unacceptably restricts his freedom to have and do anything he wants, any time he wants.

Violent Past

The Dyssocial has a history of frequent violence. He is much more combative than the Asocial. He has a short temper and depends upon violence to intimidate people or to eliminate the slightest antagonism. His violence is spontaneous, with complete disregard for the consequences. He does not internalize frustration, as does the Asocial, but he vents it as it forms, or as soon after as opportunity will permit. He is a vocal and physical bully, unlike the quiet, inexpressive Asocial.

Self-Importance

His lack of ability to conform to social norms makes this person a social misfit. He is hedonistic, thinking only on the basis of current desires and emotions, and he acts on them immediately. As the Asocial was respectful of authority but easily alienated by a sense of unfairness, this person has no respect for any form of authority or for anyone else's rights or interests. It is his character and personality to be selfish, challenging, and argumentative on a regular basis, and with little or no provocation.

Power Assertiveness

This person has a history of bullying and intimidating people in order to have his own way. He is likely to intimidate co-workers or supervisors of either sex, verbally or physically. He believes his best defense is a good offense. Johnny W. Burns, mentioned above and in Chapter 1, had such a history of violence. Thomas McIlvane, the Royal Oak postal employee, had a history of threatening supervisors. He had been brought to trial for making threats over the telephone but was ultimately acquitted of those charges. Generally, he was unfriendly, disagreeable, argumentative, demanding, uncompromising, and threatening—a definitive portrait of a power-assertive personality.

Substance Abuse

The Asocial type may abuse alcohol or drugs, but it is more an aggravating factor than a causal factor, as is the case with the Dyssocial. The Dyssocial tends more often than the Asocial to abuse substances while on the job.

Weapons

He is prone to carrying weapons on a regular basis, on the job or elsewhere. He has less fascination and less psychological dependence on weapons than the Asocial does. Instead, he sees them as a tool for spontaneous protection or enforcement of his wishes or desires.

Criminal Record

The Dyssocial is likely to have been involved in a variety of illegal behaviors and to have an arrest record. Even though both types have violent pasts, the Dyssocial is more prone to criminality as a lifestyle of choice than is the Asocial. His criminal past is marked by more proactive criminal intent than is that of the Asocial, whose arrests more often were due to reactions rather than intentional actions.

Manipulation

The Dyssocial person believes he has the power and ability to make things happen for his benefit, but he uses guile, deceit, and power to do so. When these do not work, he switches to power to manipulate events. If neither works, and he is put off by another's strong personality, particularly one with authority, he backs off and plans a tactical response, which may include violence. If he is able to hold his temper, he then plans, waits for the proper moment, and acts. This planned event is not spontaneous and outrageous, but tactical. He carefully measures where and when to act in order to maximize effect and avoid response by authorities. If he is unable to control his temper, he forces a confrontation, even violently. A nonunion organization would probably fire him at this point, but if he is a union member, unless there is serious injury resulting from his actions, he would likely be disciplined but would probably continue employment.

Mentally Ill

Mental disorders may be the genesis of some violent behaviors in the workplace. More often, they are an aggravating factor. When people are undergoing significant, persistent frustration, they attempt to unload it somewhere. There are three ways in which they commonly attempt to do so.

First, they turn the frustration inwardly against themselves. The effect of this approach is the manifestation of psychophysiologic disorders—actual physical manifestations of pathologies with psychological origins. Examples are:

- Skin disorders such as hives, boils, and rashes
- Somatic, or body function, disorders related to eating, sleeping, sex, or waste eliminations and control
- Consequent weight losses or gains
- Ulcers
- Ulcerated colitis
- Sexual frigidity or impotence
- Headaches and other aches and pains

Second, they may choose to unload their frustrations by taking them out on inanimate objects, i.e., displacing the emotions. Many people vent their frustration on things. Unfortunately, there are some people who do it more often than others. Some even become dependent upon this type of overt activity to unload the buildup of their frustrations. This activity can sometimes be of a serious and dysfunctional nature.

Third, and the one most pertinent to this book, is the venting of frustrations on other people. This method of unloading one's frustrations is obviously the most dangerous. If the mentally ill perceive that their co-workers, bosses, or subordinates are their antagonists, they may choose to vent their frustrations upon them.

The definition of mental stability is abstract. One definition asserts that it is the frequency and quality with which one is able to react to all of life's stimuli with highly appropriate and effective behaviors, measured on a continuum from 0 to 100%. There is no magic point along the continuum at which one is labeled as stable or unstable. The measure of "quality" of reaction gauges both appropriateness and effectiveness. For example, one might behave 95% of the time with a quality rating of 4+ for appropriate and effective responses. Another might behave 90% of the time with 3+ for appropriate and effective responses. There are no definitive criteria by which to measure mental stability, except to say that it is roughly the frequency with which one behaves highly appropriately and effectively to the widest range of life's stimuli. The manner of inappropriateness often takes on common forms, and the attendant degrees of ineffectiveness combine with frequency of episodes to constitute diagnoses of mental disorders.

When barriers or obstacles get in the way of need satisfaction, one is frustrated. The nature of the need, the strength of its demand, the lack of any perceived opportunity to detour around the barrier to obtain satisfaction, and the length of time the frustration has persisted combine to influence the person's resultant behavior formation. People's basic needs are so powerful and demanding that those who cannot satisfy them legally, morally, and realistically may resort to illegal, immoral, and/or unrealistic behaviors for satisfaction. Two approaches to dealing with frustrations are (1) to confront them, or "fight" to alter or destroy them, or (2) to "flee" to another environment where the barrier is less evident or nonexistent. These two approaches are commonly known collectively as the "fight or flight" syndrome. Fortunately, most people who become mentally unstable or unbalanced tend to choose the "flight" approach in dealing with their frustrations. However, even they, once they perceive that fleeing does not appear to work or that they have no other choice, may choose to alter their approach and "fight."

Mentally stable people have a variety of ways of coping with frustrations by compromising the appropriateness and effectiveness of their responses to frustration, to avoid either side of the fight or flight syndrome. Instead of exhibiting a normal 4+ behavior in dealing with a particular frustration, they may compromise and react with a 2+ appropriate and effective response, thereby achieving some degree of satisfaction without having to fight or flee. Some people never learn how or when to use these compromises, however. Consequently, they must resort to the extreme behaviors of fighting or fleeing. Most often, they learn to flee physically and psychologically. However, as previously stated, when fleeing does not work, fighting is the other alternative. This most aptly describes the Asocial type, described above. The Dysocial type, by contrast, depends first on fighting.

Personality Disorders

As previously discussed, personality disorders are learning disorders that become habits. These habits become part of one's personality. If one's habits are generally functional within their host culture, they are desirable. However, when habits are generally dysfunctional, they are labeled as personality disorders.

Some examples of personality disorders are described in the following sections.

Schizoid Personality

"Schizoid" derives from the Greek word meaning "to split," indicating a split from interaction with other people and their common culture. This person is a loner, preferring to work alone and not take part in social activities. By separating himself from others, he becomes out of sync with dominant social norms; he no longer knows how to act with and react to other people, especially in strained or challenging situations.

H. Lang, the La Porte city employee, is a good example of this type.

Impulse Control Disorder (Intermittent Explosive Disorder)

This type has a low tolerance for frustration, is easily provoked, and quickly loses his temper. He then strikes out against his perceived antagonist. This person may appear to be normal in all other fashions and effective in achievement of work tasks; however, he misinterprets others' intentions, even harmless jokes, taking them seriously and personally. He is territorial, possessive, and sensitive to criticism.

Passive–Aggressive Personality

One might label him with the "spoiled child syndrome," as he never learned either to delay gratification or to *earn* anything. Everything was always given to him whenever he wanted it by his caretakers. He never learned that the world requires him to create or produce what he gets— that when he becomes an adult, no one will be serving his every wish with no effort required on his part. He may have a proper value system otherwise intact. He generally knows right from wrong, but he has never correctly learned the system of effort and reward. Consequently, when he enters adulthood and is expected to provide and care for himself, he does not know how. He thinks the least amount of effort on his part is significant; to ask any more of him would be unreasonable. He has learned to be passive and still be rewarded.

On the job, he becomes easily angered when not rewarded for what he views as considerable effort but what his supervisor and co-workers see as inadequate. Additionally, when he is asked for more effort, he sees it as a gross and unfair expectation and feels he is being taken advantage of. Since he has not learned otherwise, he feels righteously justified in striking out against such provocation. He is so dysfunctional at work that he generally does not last a long time on any job without becoming threatening or violent.

Paranoid Personality

This person has a general attitude that no one likes him and that people intentionally annoy or interfere with him. People around him become tired of being accused of scheming against him and begin to avoid him. Unfortunately, this merely fulfills his expectations of them. This feeds into a dangerous, negative, cause-and-effect spiral that can lead to violence.

Anti-Social Personality

Formerly known as a psychopathic or sociopathic personality, this person is characterized as having several symptoms of maladaptive learning. First, he has failed to fully develop an internal value system, or conscience. Therefore, he has no interest in adhering to social or legal restrictions on his desires or behaviors. Second, he has learned to be extremely self-centered, with no feeling or caring for anyone else. Third, although he may have learned some degree of delayed gratification, he never learned why it was delayed. If he wants something that is accessible in any manner, he feels it should be all right for him to take it.

He fights, take chances, demands mental or physical excitement, and is unable to withstand tedium and boredom. He shows signs of personal distress, complains, and whines about any sign of aggressiveness directed at him by someone else. He does not build; he just tears down. He does not produce; he only consumes. He is a parasite, thriving on the product of others. He avoids the strong and preys on the weak. He either dominates or destroys, and when he cannot, he runs. This personality is sometimes shared by the Asocial.

The Dyssocial is a loquacious, confident conman, using force and intimidation if deception and promises will not suffice. He tends to attract a following of lesser personalities, together comprising a "gang" who can do his bidding and enforce his threats and demands. When the Asocial shares this personality, he is lacking in confidence, verbal skills, and interpersonal skills, is more passive, and attracts no following. The Dyssocial is combative whereas the Asocial is sneaky. Both are vengeful. Neither ever believes himself to be wrong, always blaming others, even his victims. Both are deceitful and inveterate liars, the Dyssocial being the more skilled of the two.

Narcissistic Personality Disorder

This person exhibits an insatiable need to gain attention and admiration from others. He is totally self-absorbed, believing himself to be particularly attractive and likeable. He expects others to treat him as special and to bestow upon him favors and considerations. When criticized, he feels intense rage and may launch a violent attack.

Neurotic and Psychotic Disorders

As the personality disorders were maladaptive learning disorders, the classifications of neuroses and psychoses are mood and/or "thinking" disorders. The greatest distinction between the two is that the psychotic has a break with reality; he experiences episodes wherein he cannot differentiate reality from fantasy. His behavior while in a psychotic episode is generally more dysfunctional than that of neurotic behaviors.

NEUROTIC DISORDERS

Two of the most common neurotic disorders are depressive neuroses and anxiety neuroses. Although these conditions alone seldom generate violence in the workplace, frustrations can build up in other areas of the sufferer's life, and some event in the workplace ultimately can set him off.

A disorder more likely to cause violence in the workplace is an obsessive–compulsive neurosis. Obsessions are recurring, uncontrollable thoughts or patterns of thoughts. Compulsions are recurring, uncontrollable patterns of behavior, usually related to the obsessions. In extreme cases, there are even criminal behaviors attendant to this condition. Power and control are two of the most powerful psychological constructs. When one perceives a loss of either, let alone both, it significantly interrupts mental stability and demands reinstatement, realistically or via one of the classical defense mechanisms. The resultant effect on the person's everyday affairs is an overcontrolling of all functions deemed important in life. He becomes very fastidious, requiring everything to be in order and under control. At work, he is very boundary conscious and protective. Trespassers elicit angry rebukes and warnings. Repeated transgressions are bound to provoke increasingly stronger responses. He is often seen by coworkers as being very uptight.

PSYCHOTIC DISORDERS

The most significant characteristic of psychotic behavior is that it is so bizarre that it cannot be overlooked. The most deceptive characteristic of the disorder is that, among some people, it appears episodically. While not in episode, the psychotic functions normally, and no one suspects a problem; when in episode, however, his behavior is noticeably dysfunctional. A psychotic exhibiting otherwise normal behavior can unexpectedly manifest quite abnormal behavior when an episode is triggered by frustrating events in the workplace. Often, people who are psychotic but not in episode tend not to take their preventive medications, thinking they do not need them. The failure to do so makes another episode even more likely.

Simple Schizophrenia—The schizophrenic usually does not become violent, but there are exceptions. He fits into the Asocial typology: he is the ultimate loner, unable to work closely with others. He is very quiet, reclusive, nonassertive, noncompetitive, and unable to handle criticism.

Paranoid Schizophrenia—While in episode, the paranoid schizophrenic is extremely dysfunctional in the workplace. Although he seldom remains employed long enough to cause problems, this is not *always* true. Prime examples of paranoid schizophrenic behavior in the cases cited in Chapter 1 were Joseph Wesbecker, at the Louisville Standard Gravure, and Robert Wickes, the Brentwood, New York, schoolteacher who took a class at his old school hostage and shot one of the students before killing himself.

People with this kind of psychosis have delusions of persecution; they have unrealistic perceptions of events and relationships, believing that someone or a group of people is intentionally persecuting them. Commonly, they live in the worlds of fantasy and reality at the same time, able to function generally but distracted and diverted by their preoccupation with perceived plots of persecutors. When they strike out, they believe that they do so in righteous self-defense. Paranoid schizophrenics may also suffer from delusions of grandeur. When this is the case, they believe that they are heroes, ridding the world of an undesirable person or group of people.

They are obvious enough in their delusional focuses that employers and co-workers should be able to recognize them as such. Employers then should channel them back into familial custody for treatment or refer them to the company Employee Assistance Program.

Bipolar Disorder (Manic–Depressive Psychosis)—The bipolar disorder is characterized by episodes of depression followed by episodes of mania, or hyperexcitability. The mixed, or cyclical, type of bipolar switches frequently between the two moods. Some remain in one or the other the majority of the time. When in either type of episode, this person is not very functional in the workplace, and he is not likely to be able to remain in a job very long. It is common enough, however, so that an awareness of it on the part of employers is prudent.

While in the depressed state, the manic–depressive is likely to be suicidal. He may view death as the only place to find peace, and if so, he is not unwilling to take someone else there with him.

While in the manic state, he has very unrealistic and exaggerated plans for the future. He has exceeding stamina in all physical and mental activity, although the mental activity is not very logical. He is very easily frustrated and can become aggressive. He is unwilling to face the reality of things but willing to fight to protect his delusion of future plans.

General Symptoms of Mental Disorders

As previously discussed, there are great numbers of mentally ill people who have entered the American workplace, particularly in the last 30 years. These people are unable to cope with various sources of frustration, many of which emanate from the workplace. Several of the individuals previously cited in the cases in Chapter 1 obviously had difficulty in interpreting the reality of situations. They had trouble forming appropriate and effective responses to life's stimuli, thereby resorting to the unrealistic, inappropriate, and ineffective alternative of violence.

Generally, people with mental disorders have some combination of the following:

- **Mood swings**—Extreme variations in mood without obvious or reasonable reasons.
- **Paranoid behavior**—Delusions (false, distorted, or unrealistic beliefs) of grandeur, believing oneself to be someone special or a famous person. If a paranoid person believes that someone, or a group of people, is persecuting him, he becomes increasingly dangerous as he dwells on the perceived threat. Initially, he concentrates on his persecutors and on the nature of the persecution. Eventually, his thoughts and/or expressions take on a violent theme, which becomes more detailed and specific as time goes by. Finally, he focuses on his persecutors as the targets of this intended violence.
- **Depression**—All mentally ill persons have episodes of depression, whether they be significant and prolonged, significant but episodic, mild but prolonged, or mild and episodic. Depression is characterized by apathy, perpetual sadness, social withdrawal, reduced effectiveness, unrealistic expectations, unkempt physical appearance, poor hygiene, and feelings of hopelessness, despair, helplessness, and powerlessness. It is estimated that one in every four women and one in every ten men will experience clinical depression sometime during their lifetime.
- **Anxiety**—This is the inability to find mental peace due to underlying, sometimes unrecognized, frustrations and fears. Associated behaviors are obvious

physical uneasiness, specific or general apprehension, and the inability to concentrate.

- **Hallucinations**—False or distorted sensory perceptions, i.e., seeing, tasting, touching, smelling, or hearing things that do not exist.
- **Talking to themselves or hearing voices**—A great number of normal people talk to themselves, but the difference is that normal people know that they are doing so. They know that it is themselves to whom they are muttering and that there are no real voices replying. A mentally ill person does not know it is himself with whom he is speaking or that the voices he hears are only in his mind.
- **Self-punishment or self-destruction**—Harming of his own body, sometimes accompanied by suicidal tendencies.
- **Unrealistic physical complaints**—The person may take excessive sick leave, particularly when no ailment can be identified, other than one that is psychosomatic. There may also be a history of excessive workers' compensation claims and constant complaints of aches and pains. Sometimes, however, the person may in fact manifest symptoms of skin disorders, intestinal or bowel disorders, or weight problems.
- **Disruptions of habit**—Abnormal patterns of eating, sleeping, working, sexual appetite and capabilities, or bodily functions.

The more of these symptoms an employee possesses, the more likely the person is to act out violently. Whether or not this happens can depend upon how many other problems pile up from various aspects of the employee's life at any given time. If the use of alcohol and/or other chemicals is combined with any one or more of these typologies, it tends to increase the overall potential for violent behavior. In counseling individuals with substance abuse problems, the authors have found that alcohol and drugs create a profound negative effect on one's inability to cope with problems. Which came first—the problems or the dependency on chemical substances—does not seem to matter. The foreign substances have the effect of diminishing one's ability to form appropriate and effective responses to problems. Therefore, old problems go unsolved. Feeble attempts to solve them, or to ignore them, usually complicate the problems, causing new ones. The increased number and gravity of problems stimulate a greater use and dependency upon the substances of choice. Frustrations mount, and the probability of desperate, excessively violent behavior increases.

When there is a build-up of personal problems, the primary source of which may not even be in the place of employment, the person also begins to exhibit the described typologies *in* the workplace. This inability to solve problems may be compounded by an inability to find someone in the organization to understand his viewpoint, which leaves the employee in a state of perceived powerlessness. Should the employee decide to regain that power by eliminating the cause(s) of the problem(s), he becomes very focused and mission-oriented, righteous in his justifications, and consequently very difficult to reach with logic and reason.

A good example of someone in this state of mind is Stephen Leith, the Chelsea teacher. By the account of his wife, it was obvious he was determined to kill the superintendent. He was so focused on this mission that there was no one who could stop him at that point. He was willing to sacrifice himself in the service of his mission to see his sense of justice prevail.

Summarizing the Typologies

The more of the above traits and behaviors that are exhibited by a person, the greater his inability to meet and effectively deal with adverse events and circumstances. Even if a person had *all* of the above traits and behaviors, it is not a certainty, not even a probability, that this person is foreordained to behave violently. However, of those who *have* already acted out violently in the workplace, *all* of them exhibited at least some or more of the typologies of the mentally ill. These typologies, then, can function as flags to catch the attention of employers and employees. They are thereby alerted to the fact that the person is a potential threat and may be in need of counseling or psychiatric treatment. Supervisors and fellow employees who observe these behaviors should notify their organizational personnel crisis coordinator. If no such person has been designated by the organization, then they should report it to their supervisor with recommendations for action.

Each organization, however, should designate a personnel crisis coordinator who is trained to make judgments on how reports of violence or potential violence should be handled. Organizations should promulgate rules and regulations prohibiting harassment, threats, or assaults of any kind and require that such incidents be reported to the crisis coordinator. This rule should apply to all levels of the organization and be universally and uniformly enforced. Such action is required to satisfy an employer's legal obligation to protect its employees and customers. All personnel, therefore, should be given training in the recognition of these typologies and their origins.

5

FACTORS CONTRIBUTING TO WORKPLACE VIOLENCE

Theory X and Theory Y

The late Douglas McGregor introduced a powerful analysis of management styles and managers' attitudes regarding the nature of people as workers, which he called "assumptions." McGregor claimed that these assumptions dictate the style of management managers employ. Because McGregor did not want to imply any value judgments in his observations, he labeled the two sets of assumptions as *Theory X* and *Theory Y*.

Theory X, he stated, implied an autocratic or authoritative approach to managing people. Theory X assumed:

- People dislike work and will try to avoid it if at all possible.
- People are not willing to make an effort at work because they are lazy.
- People have little ambition and, if they can, will avoid all responsibility.
- People are self-centered, indifferent to organizational needs, and very resistant to change. The only way that

management can get a high level of performance from people is to coerce, control, and threaten them.

McGregor observed that Theory X was not consistent with what the science of psychology had found in the past 70 years regarding the nature of people, which findings he labeled Theory Y. According to Theory Y, people are not lazy. Laziness grew out of workers' experiences with organizations and their managers' expectations and treatment of them. If managers were to provide the proper environment, employees could realize their full potentials. Work would become as natural as play or rest, and workers would exercise self-direction and self-control to achieve organizational goals and objectives to which they had become committed.

McGregor's argument was that since managers had long been following a false set of assumptions about people, they actually had been mismanaging people, leaving them unfulfilled, frustrated, and even angry in their jobs. Many organizations continue to coerce, threaten, and discipline employees to get them to work and conform to organizational rules and regulations. These organizations are neither psychologically healthy nor stable work environments. The authors believe the violence-prone organization is the one that still uses this Theory X management.

Even organizations that have been enlightened to Theory Y may still have managers who believe and use the guidelines of Theory X. These managers do not have effective people skills and often harass employees by using psychologically threatening behaviors. Obviously, employees dislike these managers and often find a way to retaliate in some manner. They may not use violence against other employees, but they may destroy equipment, lower their productivity, and value nonproductive behavior. Managers who employ the Theory X management style assume either a militaristic or paternalistic attitude. They think they have absolute control over the lives of the employees they manage. Supervisors employing these destructive tactics believe they must be right at all costs—and the costs are disgruntled, alienated, even hostile employees. In most cases, these supervisors are very difficult to change. Most often they do not see any need to change, because they believe they have had a great deal of success using the Theory X style.

Some comments from postal service managers and employees exemplify these frustrations. An article in the *Baltimore Sun* on May, 11, 1993 reported, "Often, Postal Service managers are disgruntled themselves and show little concern for the plight of their workers." Said a postal clerk in Philadelphia speaking about treatment by supervisors and managers, "It can make you crazy." Former Postmaster General Anthony M. Frank stated that many managers maintain an attitude toward their subordinates best illustrated by the comment, "I ate dirt for 20 years, and now it's your turn to eat dirt."

Although it may be difficult to identify the behaviors of supervisors as direct causes of employee violence, they certainly contribute to the problem.

Employee Performance Appraisals

Supervisors' past performance evaluations can be highly stressful to subordinates as well as to supervisors, especially in a Theory X organization. The stakes are very high, as employees' futures are on the line. The possibility of receiving negative feedback makes employees apprehensive, fearful, and defensive. Unfortunately, most performance evaluations are based upon subjective rather than objective data. Rated employees see it as a personal judgment rather than as a fair, impersonal one. Such resentment may be exacerbated if the employee has received no other feedback, whether positive or negative, from the manager during the time period being evaluated. Employees want to feel they have some control over their own jobs; in such a situation they feel robbed of this control, which is both frustrating and aggravating.

Often, the appraisal is not used to rate the employee's professional development, but for personnel actions such as rewards, transfers, or even termination. Employees may not even be told how the data was gathered or what the performance criteria were.

Some supervisors/managers do not like to evaluate their subordinates and feel threatened by the process. They believe they are being asked to be the judge, coach, friend, *and* manager of their subordinates, which places them in a position of role conflict. Although they might be inclined to award higher overall ratings, their own supervisors often have instructed them not to award very many ratings above the mid-range—mediocre or satisfactory. The evaluations the supervisor actually reports then become meaningless and unfounded, yet the supervisor must defend them.

Another pitfall attendant upon the subjectivity of employee performance appraisals has been dubbed the halo effect. This refers to one positive—or negative—characteristic about an employee that colors all of the other impressions the supervisor has about that employee.

Other problems that contribute to the subjectivity of appraisals arise from the managers themselves. Some supervisors try to avoid any conflict in the appraisal by rating everyone "average," no matter what they deserve. Others give all employees favorable ratings, while others generally appraise their subordinates unfavorably. Employee appraisals historically seem to have reflected managers' adoption of a Theory X attitude about their subordinates. Such appraisals are used to keep people in line and to make sure they are working hard.

Past performance appraisals should be used primarily as a tool for employees' professional development. Evaluation data must be gathered on a regular basis throughout the rating period, and employees should fully understand the criteria of performance and behavior upon which they are being judged. Supervisors who give appraisals can be trained to overcome some of the subjectivity problems in their administration.

In theory, appraisals would seem to be a positive management tool to improve and maintain performance. A fair and valid appraisal system can prevent employee hostility. Poor evaluations, however, can have an aggravating effect, especially upon an already unstable person. For example, on July 19, 1995, a city electrician in Los Angeles, angered over a poor performance evaluation, shot to death four supervisors.

Effects of Stress (Distress)

Peggy Lawless, a research project director for Northwestern National Life, was quoted in *USA Today* as stating that people who feel high levels of stress on the job are nearly two times more likely to become violent than unstressed workers. Although stress can be generated by an authoritarian style of management, there are innumerable other sources of stress in the workplace. Although many can be readily identified, and employees can be taught how to eliminate, reduce, avoid, or manage stress, often it goes undetected until its symptoms become manifest in some employee's hostile behavior.

Psychologist Hans Selye defined stress as the "wear and tear on the body caused by life." While awake, everyone is under some degree of stress. The only complete escape is death. Unfortunately, some highly stressed employees may consider just that as a way out.

There are good forms of stress (eustress) and bad forms (distress). When people are asked to describe their own stress, they often describe it as an "emotional, unpleasant state." According to Selye, when an external stimulus is perceived as significantly threatening, certain natural, autonomic (uncontrollable) physiological responses occur, each of which is stressful. If the stressor persists, stress turns into distress. This phenomenon can be divided into distinct stages:

- **Alarm stage**—When people are confronted with any threat to their safety or well-being, they experience an immediate and vigorous alarm reaction. This stage is known as the *flight or fight response,* previously mentioned, in which people prepare to either run or stay and fight. In this stage, there are many attendant physiological reactions accompanying psychological fear.
- **Resistance stage**—The initial alarm reaction is soon replaced by both psychological and physiological resistance. The activation of the body remains relatively high for awhile, but drops to a level more sustainable over a long period of time.
- **Exhaustion stage**—If the stress persists, the person's resources become depleted and the mental and physical ability to cope decreases sharply. If the stress persists for an even longer period, severe biological and psychological impairment usually occurs.

Distressful situations seem to share the following properties:

- Stressors are so intense that they produce a state of overload, when the person can no longer adapt to them.
- They evoke simultaneous incompatible tendencies, such as the urge to confront or avoid an object, person, or activity.
- The tendencies are not controllable by the person.

Distress results from a person's cognitive appraisal of the situation as follows:

- The situation is somehow threatening to the person's important goals.

- The person is unable to cope with the situation and its dangers or demands.
- The person is overwhelmed by the events, perceiving that demands will exceed his or her personal coping resources.

In the authoritative, Theory X workplace, there are a number of situations that cause a person with a fragile personality to feel distressed:

- **Lack of social support**—When people feel they do not have the support of either their superior or their workgroup, they will experience distress.
- **Lack of participation in decisions**—People want to feel they have at least some control over their fate in the workplace and feel threatened when they do not.
- **Role conflict**—Role conflict is common in many work settings, and there is mounting evidence that it is a major cause of distress. Most people fill several roles in their lives, and they frequently find that the demands of one role conflict with those of others. Research generally indicates that the more individuals must juggle different roles, the more negative their moods seem to be.
- **Role ambiguity**—When people are uncertain about the roles they are supposed to play in their jobs or what behaviors are expected in those roles, they become unnerved and distressed.
- **Work environment**—In many work settings, there are physical conditions that can cause distress. An uncomfortable physical environment, due to heat, cold, loud noise, crowding, or poor lighting, can cause distress. A person exposed to these conditions who is experiencing stress from other sources as well can be profoundly affected by such seemingly innocuous factors.
- **Change**—Change, particularly when the end result is unknown, causes distress. A shift in company policy,

reorganization, mergers, changes in job or managers, or, worse, loss of job all generate high levels of uncertainty and therefore distress.

- **Work hours**—Long days and long weeks, particularly if prolonged, cause distress. Some companies have found that it is cheaper to work fewer people longer than to hire more of them. Over time, this wears the employee down both mentally and physically.
- **Ergonomics**—Ergonomics is the study of employees' biomechanical compatibilities, a new and growing field in industrial engineering. Evidence indicates that physical discomforts, especially any threat of danger from equipment or chemicals with which the employee must work, also contribute to stress. More and more work days are being lost to employee claims of health problems resulting from biomechanical trauma. There is ample evidence to indicate that the physical stresses from work tools and machinery, processes, movements, sounds, air, lighting, etc. can be incompatible to human welfare.

Although these environmental factors are usually not so intrusive as to constitute noticeable trauma, they are cumulative. Over a period of time, their effects become manifest in either physical and/or psychological pathologies. This process is known as cumulative trauma disorder (CTD). The effect of CTD is added distress on the job, which carries over to off-job life conduct.

To reduce employee distress, organizations should:

- Redesign employee appraisals to assist in the professional development of employees, rather then using them solely to justify adverse personnel actions.
- Set realistic workloads, work pace, and work schedules.
- Redesign jobs so they will provide a challenge to people. Most people like the feeling of responsibility and the sense of achievement.

- Train workers in the skills they need to provide some input into the decisions affecting them and the jobs they perform.
- To the maximum extent possible, allow employees some discretion about how they do their jobs.
- Be clear about work expectations, standards of performance, and the roles employees are expected to fill.
- Provide feedback to employees about their performance on a frequent basis.
- Provide training and development opportunities for employees. People who perform unchallenging work with no hope of anything better tend to feel insecure, disappointed, and isolated.
- Through sensible managerial designs, provide extra support in times that may be distressful and, in the extreme, create employee assistance programs wherein distressed employees may secure assistance.

Economic Factors That Contribute to Violence in the Workplace

Downsizing

Downsizing, the process by which organizations reduce the number of people in the workforce in order to reduce costs and increase profitability, is becoming common in today's business world. The announcement of a downsizing is very threatening because the employees know some of them are going to lose their jobs. *Job* and *security* no longer can be thought of together.

According to the September 5, 1995, issue of *Industry Week,* during 1994 U.S. companies reportedly were downsizing at a rate in excess of 2,500 employee reductions each day. This is a rate 5% higher than in 1991, when the country was still in recession. IBM reportedly has eliminated more than 100,000 jobs over the past four years. AT&T has downsized, as has General Motors. According to a study by the American Society for Quality and Productivity, 85% of the Fortune 500 companies have downsized in recent years.

Feelings of uneasiness and uncertainty are pervasive in many such workplaces. Workers ask, "Whose job is the next one to go?" Thirty years ago, an individual could start a job with a company right out of college or high school and expect to stay with it until retirement. The days of one-job-for-life are nearly gone. People who enter the job market today may change jobs as many as seven to twelve times before they retire.

Companies that downsize as a way to cut costs rarely address the emotional needs of the individuals they release. Since none of the employees know in advance who will stay and who will go, they experience a number of emotional and psychological stages:

- Denial
- Self-blame
- Anger
- Depression
- Acceptance

Employees who are terminated due to downsizing suffer lowered self-esteem and are left with a very uncertain view of the future. They may have to relocate to another city to find another job. Left behind are the extended family and friends, the support groups they need most at that time. When they do find another job, they may be very anxious, fearing that their future in the new company may be as tenuous as at the last one. They may have difficulty forming relationships at a new company. If they work alone, it may prolong their sense of abandonment, further increasing distress.

One organization told people who were being laid off that they were "surplus employees." No one wants to be thought of as "surplus." Situations like this happen because managers are not trained to handle the issuance of the notorious "pink slip." Many companies, when downsizing, plan poorly and give too little consideration to the effects on the employees being released. Their attention is focused on managing the effects on the employees remaining. No wonder a recent *Time* magazine poll showed that 70% of the U.S. workers say they do not trust *anyone.*

The authors interviewed several former employees of companies who were laid off after 25 or more years of service. Although most organizations offered early retirement to employees who were eligible, even that was sometimes handled in an insensitive manner. One person said, "When I heard they were going to offer early retirements, I was happy. I wanted to retire and do something different than I had been doing for the past 30 years. When I was called into my manager's office, I was excited, and I really felt good. The manager and the personnel director, both of whom I knew very well and had worked with closely, were there, and when they started telling me what I was going to be offered and the tone of voice they used, I was floored. I thought I had been a valued employee, but when they finished, I realized I had only been a body that had done a job. I really meant nothing to them or the organization, and it made me angry. As the meeting went on, I got more angry and couldn't believe what I was hearing. I couldn't believe how insensitive they were and how insensitive the meeting was. After the meeting [ended] and my anger subsided, I realized that the way I had been treated was probably good as compared to the people who were being terminated without the benefit of retirement."

In the November 1994 issue of the *AARP Bulletin,* an article on downsizing related anecdotes about organizations' handling of retirements and/or terminations of longtime employees. Many of these people indicated that they had left their jobs under duress. One gentleman told of being offered an early buyout, but was also told that if he did not take it, he would be laid off later with less favorable terms. Most of the people who had gone through downsizing described it as an insensitive process. All said they were hurt and angry about it.

Many downsized employees find they are not qualified to compete for a similar replacement job. Many of them were at levels of responsibility and pay at which other organizations tend not to hire from the outside. Others find that their skills are no longer in demand, and they must be retrained or go to college to learn a new profession. Because many well-paying factory jobs have been sent "offshore," and more and more downsized people are looking, competition is fierce. Some people go for months, some for even a year or more, trying to find work. Few find what they were hoping for. During their unemployment, bills may go unpaid, and the threat of loss of car or home becomes a disturbing distraction. The longer they go without work, the more desperate and angry they become.

Other factors that emerge from downsizing are the emotional trauma and increased workloads of the employees who survive personnel cuts. They experience feelings of sadness, role ambiguity, and distrust. As with the downsized employees, their self-esteem may suffer, and distress may result from long hours and increased workloads.

Most organizations manage this transition poorly and end up with a slim workforce with low morale. Employees need to be given an opportunity to vent their emotions without repercussions. Survivors of traumatic layoffs experience the same stages of grief as do employees who were laid off. Survivors sometimes take even longer periods to recover than did those who left, particularly if the others succeeded in finding new jobs. Meanwhile, survivors continue to wonder how long they will be able to stay, and they have no way to alleviate their fears.

In an American Management Association survey of 500 companies that had downsized, 75% of them reported that morale had collapsed. Some survivors are embittered enough to act out violently, yet few organizations have devised effective ways to reduce their frustrations.

Mergers and Takeovers

A generation ago, there were relatively few mergers or takeovers. Various deregulations, such as in the airlines and banking industries, and the relaxation of certain antitrust prohibitions have caused a merger and buyout frenzy. Once underway, the movement changed the cultures of many U.S. businesses forever.

Mergers and takeovers have ominous and wide-ranging implications for companies and their personnel. Particularly in the "lesser" (bought-out) organization, operational and managerial ranks may be pruned ruthlessly and the organizational culture drastically changed. It is not uncommon for employees to go to work soon after the fusion and be greeted with, "Welcome to the merger. You're fired."

Two organizations with significantly different cultures generally do not fuse well, and employees of both of the original organizations are likely to experience "cultural collision." The dominant culture attempts to impose itself onto the other, sometimes with an air of superiority. The effects on the people in the smaller organization are likely to last for a long time.

Significantly negative emotions in long-term employees of the lesser firm are often caused by decreases in their benefits package due to an attempt to bring it into alignment with that of the dominant firm. They feel that they made significant investments into the package of the old company; now, with the reduction or loss of some of their equity, they react first with disbelief and resentment, perhaps followed by grief, depression, and anger.

Often employees from both of the original organizations feel themselves to be "second-class" citizens in the
new structure. They now may have a supervisor from the
other organization who treats them differently. This gives
rise to feelings of betrayal by their old organization and
its managers, whom they believe "sold them out." Even if
the merger is considered to be friendly, the reactions to
the "culture collision" still are significant. These reactions
may never subside, and the workers may never trust or
get along with one another. These situations obviously
have the potential for creating significant distress among
employees.

Several years ago, three Delco Remy plants in Anderson, Indiana, were merged into one. Even though they
were from the same General Motors division, the three
cultures never meshed as they should have. There were
constant clashes among workers and among managers of
the different plants, creating a constantly hostile and
potentially violent atmosphere.

6

VICTIMS OF WORKPLACE VIOLENCE

Recently conducted studies indicate that 80% of all work-related murder victims are male. There are no profiles of victims because they include people of all ages, races, sexes, and nationalities. When a disgruntled employee comes in looking for revenge, often he does not discriminate between the "bad guys" and the "good guys." Although the employee may be after anyone who works in management, he may kill fellow employees as well. In many cases, the employee fires randomly, without regard to who is hit. He may not intend to kill "innocent" people, but once in action, his state of mind may make it difficult for him to discern between "innocent" and "guilty," "good" and "bad." He may be angry at everyone, since he felt betrayed by fellow employees who did not stand up with him against management. Even when a domestic dispute is the catalyst, other people not at all associated with the dispute are often harmed.

According to the National Institute for Occupational Safety and Health (NIOSH), between 1980 and 1989, 40% of all women who died in the workplace were murdered. NIOSH statistics indicate that murder is the number one cause of death on the job for women. Women are particularly vulnerable to both verbal and physical abuse from male co-workers, particularly in a male-dominated culture. One interviewee, a graduate of a university industrial management program who had worked as a line production supervisor in a major automobile manufacturing plant, indicated she was harassed and threatened so much, particularly by male employees, that she had to quit the job. She indicated that she had attempted to secure the aid of plant management, but they simply ignored the problem. It appeared to her that management did not want to irritate the union. She had no witnesses who would testify on her behalf if she attempted to sue, and she did not wish to become known as a troublemaker in the plant, which could jeopardize favorable recommendations for future jobs elsewhere. This woman had a healthy self-confidence, but it was not enough alone to combat the problem.

Sexual harassment has been occurring in the workplace ever since women entered the formerly all-male domain. Although significant attention, even federal legislation, has been directed toward the problem since the early 1970s, the problem still persists. It was most notably dramatized by the Clarence Thomas Supreme Court appointment hearings, during which he was accused by former employee Anita Hill of having sexually harassed her on the job. After the hearings, sexual harassment claims mushroomed. One survey indicated that 32% of women interviewed claimed they had been sexually harassed at work. Many sexual harassment incidents end in violent encounters, although there are no specific data to accurately indicate just how many. The harassment itself is considered by many to be a violent act.

Sexual harassment takes either of two common forms:

- *Quid pro quo*—This phrase literally means "one thing in return for another." In other words, if a woman wants to continue to work at her place of employment, be promoted, or receive some other favorable work consideration, she is informed that she must submit to a boss's sexual demands.

*   **Hostile environment**—This environment, created when something is perceived as an expression of hostility by the person experiencing it, is sometimes perpetrated by men who view women as a threat to their power. Some men create, at least verbally, a hostile work atmosphere for one or more women in that workplace to re-establish the desired balance of power.

An extreme example of on-the-job sexual harassment is rape. According to U.S. Department of Justice statistics, 7% of all rapes are committed in the workplace.

Other Victims

The people who are hurt or killed by workplace violence are not the only victims. Those who witness the violence also are victims, even though the effects may be transitory. The family and friends left behind, even the family and friends of the perpetrator, may suffer negative consequences due to the event. Co-workers must return to the workplace where they experienced trauma. For some, that is not an easy task.

Some states now require a realtor to disclose to prospective buyers that a house has been the scene of a violent death or suicide. That some people are very much affected by being at the scene of former violence no doubt prompted those laws. Similarly, returning to a workplace that was the scene of the death of friends or relatives may be quite disquieting.

Although it may not often be considered, the family and friends of the violent perpetrator are also victims. Forty percent of people who commit homicide in the workplace also commit suicide. If they do not, they will probably be tried in court, putting their family through the stress of a public trial. Family members may well be subjected to the social stigma of being related to "the crazed lunatic" who committed the terrible crime.

The organization is also a victim. It may be remembered for a long time after the event as a dangerous, undesirable place to work. Unfortunately for the U.S. Postal Service and its employees, jokes or derogatory remarks about the danger of working at or even entering a post office are common. Such an image certainly has a negative effect on the postal employees.

Victims of Threats

What percentage of workers are violent? Most authorities define harassment, verbal abuse, and threats, as well as assault, as workplace violence. Nearly all persons interviewed by the authors experienced or observed at least one example of verbal abuse or threats on the part of a fellow employee they considered to be potentially violent. One example is cited below.

An employee of a small (100 employees) medical service company in a medium-sized midwestern city expressed concern over another employee who, on several occasions, made general threats of violence to the interviewee and other employees. Examples of such threats were, "I'm going to come in here someday and blow everyone away," or "Maybe something could happen here like happened at the post office."

The threatening employee had significant mood swings, suggesting he may have been on antidepressants. He was known to be taking pain medication for an old, persistent injury. Employees generally indicated they were apprehensive about what this person might do, and several reported it to management. Management chose to do nothing about the situation, and it appeared doubtful to the interviewee that it would. Meanwhile, the employees remained in suspense. Although nothing worse may happen, such a situation does not create an atmosphere in which people do their best work.

7

STRATEGIES FOR REDUCING WORKPLACE VIOLENCE

Organizational managers have legal obligations in both violence prevention and worker protection. The federal Occupational Safety and Health Act requires employers take steps to ensure a safe and healthful workplace for employees.

Although there may be no indicators upon which managers can rely to indicate *exactly* when someone is going to become violent, several behavioral typologies of violent workers have been set forth in this volume to alert managers and fellow employees to the potential. Sometimes potential killers even make statements indicating they are planning to do something. Certainly, some kind of managerial response should be forthcoming in such instances. Not only can early intervention avoid an actual incident, but the predilection of the employee toward causing an incident might have been defused by professional treatment. However, such intervention must be achieved in a timely and proper fashion. In an interview on the "Today" show (NBC), James Allen Fox, Dean of the College of Criminal Justice at Northeastern University in Boston, warned that in some cases it may actually be dangerous to identify such person(s) and attempt intervention, as it may lead to an escalation of the planned violence.

Obviously, the more knowledge a supervisor/manager has regarding the daily behavior of employees, the better chance there is of predicting potential violent actions. This means that managers must get to know the people who report to them, their likes and dislikes, their temperaments, what motivates them, and what agitates them. While managers cannot always avoid negative stimuli in dealing with employees, at least they can become aware of what potentials are created thereby.

Workers also must become sensitive to the emotional status of their co-workers. Some organizations have instituted training in human behavior, organizational behavior, abnormal behavior, stress, and conflict-resolution skills for both managers and workers. With such training, they should be better able to recognize signal behaviors not only on the part of co-workers, but better able to recognize signs of stress and distress in themselves. Particularly as many organizations are moving away from individual workstations to team concepts, workers will be interacting even more closely than in the past. They will be required to be more alert to their group dynamics and the emotional well-being of fellow team members.

Hiring Procedures

In 1983, the Minnesota Supreme Court upheld a verdict against an apartment complex for hiring a manager who was convicted of raping a tenant. The applicant had been in prison for armed robbery, and the defendant had not checked for criminal records. The court said that it was thus "foreseeable he could commit another violent crime"; a criminal check would have disclosed the conviction and precluded employment. On one hand, civil rights activists claim that former prisoners must earn a living, and therefore their records should *not* preclude employment, whereas this state supreme court dictated they should.

To the degree that the law allows, employers should check the backgrounds of applicants. If it can be validated as a *bona fide* occupational qualification (BFOQ), checks can be made on an applicant's past court conviction record, driving record, credit history, and work history. In most states, criminal convictions are a matter of public record. Unless justified as a BFOQ, the U.S. Equal Employment Opportunity Commission (EEOC) asserts that arrest checks are illegal under Title VII of the 1964 Civil Rights Act, which states that it is unlawful for an employer to "limit, segregate, or classify employees or applicants for employment in any way that would deprive or tend to deprive any individual of employment opportunities or other adversely affect their status as an employee, because of such individual's race, color, religion, sex, or national origin." The EEOC has interpreted Title VII to mean that if any job qualification is not directly a condition of ability to perform the tasks of a specific job, it does not qualify as a legal qualification for employment. If someone has a history of violent behavior as reflected by arrest records or police service calls to domestic disturbances, these facts do not constitute a BFOQ according to the EEOC.

In its effort to prevent minority discrimination in employment, the EEOC identifies some minority groups as having a disproportionate percentage of criminal arrests and convictions. That fact, says the EEOC, makes it *de facto* discrimination to screen out an applicant for a job shoveling coal because of prior arrests for violent crimes. An additional justification is that if criminal background can be justified at all as a BFOQ, it must be based only on convictions, not on arrests. However, an arrest record of 30 arrests and one conviction, which is not all that unusual in these times, may be indicative of a problem potential greater than the one conviction would portend. The nature and severity of the criminal behavior for which the applicant was convicted, the age of the offender at the time of the offense, the date of the offense, and its relationship to the job the person is applying for all must be considered according to the EEOC.

American Airlines was sued for $12 million for negligent hiring by a woman claiming an American Airlines boarding agent in Chicago bit her during a fracas while attempting to keep her from boarding without a boarding pass. After the bite, she requested that the agent be tested for AIDS; he tested positive. She claimed that American Airlines, as the employer, should have been aware of the employee's medical condition and his violent tendencies and, therefore, the airline was liable for her injury. Although cases like this one can go against employers for not checking, new laws are being passed (e.g., the Americans with Disabilities Act) prohibiting screening inquiries regarding physical and mental disabilities, workers' compensation records, and off-duty personal activities, which can indicate applicants' ability to get along with co-workers.

"Negligent hiring" suits are becoming more common. In an increasing number of cases, employers are losing on the grounds that either they failed to investigate the applicant's background or the investigation was inadequate. Employers nearly always cite Title VII, EEOC guidelines, and the Federal Privacy Act as reasons they did not do an investigation or limited it only to specific job BFOQ's. Such a defense, however, has often been judged to be insufficient in these cases. The following case is an example.

Pinkerton's, Inc. was sued in Rhode Island for negligent hiring after one of its guards was convicted of conspiracy in the theft of $200,000 in gold owned by the Welsh Manufacturing Company, which claimed that Pinkerton's had failed to adequately check the guard's background before hiring him. Pinkerton's, however, had contacted the guard's high school principal, his supervisor at the hospital where he had been previously employed, and his superior in the U.S. Navy, all of whom had provided generally positive references. None of them had commented, however, on the guard's honesty or trustworthiness. Pinkerton's also had found no criminal record in the state of Rhode Island. The Rhode Island Supreme Court, ruling in an appeal, stated that for sensitive jobs such as a security guard, employers must do an aggressive background investigation, even if initial information is positive and does not arouse suspicions.

On the other hand, if an employer fails to investigate the background of an applicant before hiring and that employee later becomes violent toward either a co-worker or a customer, the employer is vulnerable to legal suit for failure to properly screen the employee during the applicant screening process. The plaintiff's claim that a competent investigation would have revealed the applicant's history of past violent behavior has supported judgments in the plaintiffs' favor against employers.

At this time, there are no adequate and clear guidelines by which employers may be guided in deciding how thoroughly to investigate applicants' backgrounds. The safest rule of thumb would seem to be to do more rather than less. Even when they can justify doing so, too many former employers are fearful of releasing meaningful information, because they themselves feel vulnerable to suits by their former employees for violations of assumed protection of confidentiality of their employment histories.

On January 27, 1993, Paul Calden, a Fireman's Fund employee fired ten months earlier, shot and killed three former co-workers and wounded two others. During his application process for the Fireman's Fund job, Allstate Insurance Co., a former employer, had recommended him for the job. Fireman's Fund claimed to have later determined that Allstate Insurance had full knowledge of Calden's mental instability and that he frequently carried a concealed gun while at work at Allstate, so that his potential for violence was known by Allstate when Allstate recommended Calden to Fireman's Fund.

Until the uncertainty as to how far an applicant's background should be checked is clarified, companies inevitably will play it safe and be less thorough. The result is that a significant number of violence-prone employees may be hired into the American workplace in the foreseeable future.

In the meantime, employers should obtain written consent from applicants authorizing access to past employment records and personal backgrounds. This should include:

- Performance evaluations and personnel actions from personnel records in past employments
- Authorization for past supervisors to comment regarding an applicant's qualifications and work performance
- Conviction records, credit records, and driving records
- Verification of all information furnished on the application and in all interviews conducted during the screening process
- All other pertinent information required to make a valid assessment of an applicant's suitability for employment in a specific job

Particular note should be taken of unexplained gaps of time in an applicant's background, which could indicate jail terms, mental illnesses, or other employment-precluding situations, or even short-term employments that may have been terminated because of work or behavior problems.

Applicant Testing

An employment screening test is designed to measure an applicant's knowledge, skills, abilities, capabilities, personality, and character. Personality tests are used to measure basic aspects of an applicant's personality, such as introversion, stability, and motivation. They can also be used to determine the applicant's potential for violent behavior.

Examples of personality tests used are:

- Minnesota Multiphasic Personality Inventory (MMPI and MMPI-2), which measures traits such as hypochondria, paranoia, depression, and psychopathic deviation
- Guilford–Zimmerman Temperament Survey, which measures emotional stability, such as moodiness vs. friendliness or anxiety vs. calmness
- California Psychological Inventory (CPI)

Personality tests are designed to detect predetermined, unacceptable dimensions of personality relative to the job. Whereas an applicant's propensity toward violence should be a valid screening criterion for any job in which the applicant would have contact with other people, in *Soroka v. Dayton-Hudson,* a California court held that the use of certain questions on the MMPI and CPI is discriminatory under California state law. One of the arguments against these tests, stated by the EEOC, is that these multiphasic personality tests are not valid instruments for predicting violence in the workplace. Personality tests must be administered by trained personnel and interpreted by qualified experts in order to be reliable. An additional concern regarding the use of personality tests is that applicants can be briefed on how to answer the questions, thereby potentially achieving a false positive score.

Drug Screening

As with personality/character testing, there are legal issues associated with drug testing. One issue is its validity. There have been numerous claims of inaccurate results from various drug-testing methods. Most companies employ a cheap, general screening test, and if that indicates past use, they then employ a more expensive and accurate follow-up test to verify the first one before making a selection decision. Second, there are issues of invasion of privacy, wherein the applicant claims that drug testing is a constitutionally protected and unwarranted violation of his or her expectations of privacy.

Periodic or random drug testing of employees is another sticky issue. It is generally accepted that employees whose jobs affect the public safety, such as pilots and train engineers, should be subject to periodic testing to prevent disasters. However, since substance abuse is known to be a major contribution to violent behavior in the workplace, and an employee under the influence of chemical substances must certainly experience some degree of depreciated judgment, physical ability, and work capability, it would seem logical that employers should have the right to randomly test employees. The Americans with Disabilities Act (ADA) also has implications for drug testing in that protection is given to persons who have acknowledged disabilities. Applicants who claim rehabilitation from substance abuse are protected under this law, which requires that their former dependency not be a disqualifying criterion for employment. Numerous studies have indicated, however, that there is a significantly high rate of recidivism in substance abuse. In such instances, there is a likelihood of the problem becoming manifest once again before an employer can intervene.

Interviewing

The interview is both the most popular applicant screening device and, often, one of the most subjective. Interviews are critical and should be conducted by well-trained professionals. The more highly trained the interviewer, the more objective the evaluation of the results should be. As with the governance of other screening devices, the EEOC prohibits interview inquiries into any areas of one's person or background except as justifiable as a BFOQ. It is difficult to come to a strictly objective assessment of what should constitute a BFOQ, because there are legitimate work-related considerations that extend beyond the simple performance of the tasks of a job. The range of that extension is a matter of subjective judgment, a significant degree of which the employer may wish to determine.

Critical personality and character faults are not easily detected. All potential employees ought to be interviewed in depth. If possible, more than one interview should be conducted by different interviewers. Even qualified interviewers may arrive at somewhat different conclusions, which can then be compared to arrive at a fair and objective consensus.

Many organizations utilize low-paid personnel specialists who are untrained or insufficiently trained to properly make the critical assessments required to effectively screen out problem applicants. Employers who recognize the importance of this function, not only in regard to the potential for violence in employees but in regard to all other aspects of on-the-job behavior, utilize effective screening procedures and hire qualified people to administer them. Many employers understand neither the gravity of the employee selection process nor the qualifications required of its administrators.

There are open-ended questions some interviewers use to elicit projections of an applicant's personality or character that the applicant may not divulge in response to direct questions. Some examples are:

1. Describe a past situation in which you felt you were treated unfairly by a supervisor or an employer.

2. Explain why the supervisor/employer treated you in such a way.
3. Describe how you reacted to the situation.
4. Explain why you think your reaction was proper.
5. How do you think the supervisor/employer should have handled the situation?
6. How did you feel and what was your attitude about the situation when it was over?
7. Was there any other way you would have preferred to have reacted to the situation?
8. Was this situation an isolated incident or has something similar happened at other times or with other employers?
9. What do you think the probabilities are that such a problem could occur in our organization should you get the job? If that should happen, how would you anticipate handling it?
10. Have you ever had a similar problem with a fellow employee?
    (Follow with a similar series of questions.)

The following cautions should be observed:

- Both the interviewer and interviewee's mood, feelings, or physical condition may have an effect on the reliability of the data gathered from a single interview.
- If the interview is not comprehensive, the interviewee's responses may reveal only a small part of his or her possible future behaviors.

Using questions similar to those above to more carefully screen job applicants may keep potentially violent workers out of the workplace. Still, it is important to be aware of the possibility that there may already be employees with violent tendencies in the workplace, working next to the people they may eventually attack. Employers should be sufficiently in touch with long-time employees, as well as new hires, to be able to identify and defuse potentially violent behaviors before they get out of hand.

Layoff and Termination Procedures

Another strategy for reducing the chances that violence may occur is to change layoff and termination procedures. Many organizations do not have a specific process for these potentially dangerous situations. The layoff/termination processes should include the following:

1. Do not terminate an employee on a Friday. The person will not have the ability to appeal to anyone in the organization until Monday, and over the weekend, the person's frustration can build into desperation, hostility, revenge, or a perverse sense of injustice.
2. Particularly after layoffs, offer outplacement services to employees immediately. The chance to talk to someone about the possibility of future employment diminishes the feeling of desperation.
3. Offer the terminated person a chance for retraining. This option provides an identifiable goal and a specific plan for solving the problem, which is a significant alternative to what otherwise may seem to be a hopeless situation.
4. Train all personnel in the organization who may have the authority to lay off or discharge a person how to use positive language when performing these functions. When a person is being terminated, the following steps should be taken:
   - Create a structured exit interview and practice beforehand what is to be said to the employee during the termination.
   - Be careful to compose the interview using language that will create the most positive effect and reduce the potential for misunderstanding. There have been too many instances in which a manager was so vague in explaining the purpose and intention that the employee accepted it as a disciplinary action and returned to work the next day. Needless to say, when the manager had to sit down with the em-

ployee a second time, it was much more difficult to manage the termination positively, with twice the potential for resentment on the part of the employee.

- Provide a very specific reason(s) to the employee for why the action is being taken. Do not make the list of reasons too long, unless each one of them was properly addressed at the time the incident occurred. In other words, do not let a list of unattended offenses build up and then unload them on the employee at the time of termination. The employee would justifiably be resentful that such offenses had not been brought up at the time, so that they might have been addressed in order to avoid this outcome. Do not, under any circumstances, argue or negotiate the reasons for the termination.

- Do not expect a terminated employee to act rationally. Employees may react with a great deal of anger and immediately become confrontational. They often deny the act of termination is taking place. It is not unusual for such employees—both men and women—to become hysterical and cry. In other cases, they may react with hopeless resignation and immediately fall into depression. If the manager is ill-prepared to deal with any of these situations, it can aggravate rather than mitigate the situation.

- Treat all employees with objectivity, but also with respect and dignity. When a manager vents anger or frustration regarding an employee's past errant behaviors during a termination, the manager is "loading" the situation with emotionality that is almost certain to be returned in kind by the employee at some point. Treat the person as an equal, and make the person feel that he or she has been treated fairly by the company. Use *genuine* compassion. If the employee is not deserving of compassion, then simply be objective.

- Have ready at the termination all of the necessary forms required for the employee to sign and all literature explaining benefits. It is very demeaning for an employee to have to wait while the manager goes to get the papers for dismissal.
- Have the employee remove all personal belongings from the premises. Do not let the employee leave something that will provide an excuse to return. In rare cases, if a terminated employee must return to the premises, the visit should be in the company of security personnel.
- Have the employee's last paycheck prepared for delivery at the exit interview so there will be no need to return to the premises later to pick it up.
- Retrieve all devices for ingress or egress onto company premises charged to the employee, such as keys and company identification card. In some cases, if all of the keys are not retrieved, it may be necessary to change the locks. Changing locks is often considered to be too expensive, especially when minimal risk is involved, but losing such a gamble can obviously be even more expensive.
- If the layoff or discharge meeting is determined to be a "high-risk" situation, a professional counselor, such as an Employee Assistance Program counselor, should be available to counsel the person immediately after the meeting.
- If any threats are made during the meeting, they should be reported immediately after the meeting to senior managers, who should initiate appropriate contingency risk-management procedures.
- Consider giving the employee a fair separation stipend, such as is given to executives, to support the person through a reasonable period of job hunting. Such a practice may seem to be an expensive proposition, but it could save much more money in costs

related to an act of violence. Besides alleviating hardship, it shows good faith on the part of the employer and may reduce anger and frustration, in some cases enough to shortstop a possible violent response.

Addressing Personnel Problems

Unfortunately, too many managers are reluctant to proactively confront personnel problems, hoping that they will go away without their intervention. Problems left to smolder unattended, however, often unexpectedly flash into a blaze from an insignificant little spark. Confronting problems promptly and properly reduces the potential for actual incidents.

Managers need training in dispute resolution and conflict management, even in the course of their day-to-day activities, let alone in crisis situations. In fact, if managers positively resolve the day-to-day disputes, the larger problems can often be forestalled. Small problems may be the fuel for larger problems, but they can also be viewed as learning opportunities, chances for management to improve and refine problem-solving skills. However, a manager lacking such skills has the potential to improperly handle and therefore aggravate a situation instead of resolve it.

Proper documentation of events and management's response is mandatory. This is necessary both for legal purposes and for the more immediate and practical purpose of having an accurate record of events to refer to in continuing efforts to resolve the matter. Only the specific problem that occurred should be addressed; there is no need to include other events involving that employee unless they have a bearing on the event at hand.

Each organization should set up a personnel crisis center to act as a central reporting point. This center should create employee assistance programs, administered by the personnel crisis coordinator, that are prepared to handle early intervention into potential employee problems. Those who staff this crisis center, in particular, as well as all personnel in the workplace, should be trained to recognize the behavioral typologies of potentially violent people.

Finally, the organization should promulgate specific organizational rules and regulations prohibiting harassment, threats, and verbal or physical intimidation. Sanctions for such behavior must be stated explicitly, and any employee who has knowledge of such events should be required to report it, or face sanctions for not having done so. Employees should also be encouraged to report signs of potentially violent behavioral typologies in fellow workers.

Discipline

One of the dictionary definitions of "to discipline" is "to correct." There are two types of discipline, positive and negative. Both are intended to be corrective, but they are to be used in response to different situations.

Positive discipline follows positive, well-intentioned effort by employees and is intended to utilize constructive criticism and positive reinforcement to elicit or encourage desirable behaviors. Negative discipline is the response to intentional, negative commissions or omissions of behavior and involves negative criticism, directive remedies, withholding of reinforcements, and sanctions for repeated behaviors. Too often in the past, managers have wrongly viewed positive efforts resulting in less than complete success as "failure"; by definition in the old paradigm of management, failure was to result in discipline or punishment. Discipline, therefore, was only viewed as punishment.

Punishment has two negative connotations that render the concept destructive in managerial applications. First, attitudes toward punishment are grounded in the parent–child relationship, making the interchange between manager and employee seem to be a paternalistic relationship that is demeaning to the employee. Second, administering punishment can create a personal antagonism between manager and employee. Unlike sanctions, punishment cannot be viewed as impersonal. Punishment and sanctions may be virtually the same thing in fact, but in name and manner of application can differ enough to result in different psychological effects. Both are designed to make negative behaviors cost-ineffective, but impersonal sanctions have a better chance of success.

Positive Discipline

Some suggestions for the administration of positive discipline are as follows:

1. Focus on the behavior rather than on the person or the person's character, which stimulates an emotional response.
2. Do not allow the disciplinary session to become an argument. Arguments almost always end with hard feelings and no real, lasting resolution of the original problem(s). In most cases of employee violence, the worker pointed to the way management handled some prior situation, especially how management handled the employee personally. Sometimes this treatment is the very spark that triggered a violent incident.
3. Listen to the employee's complaints and viewpoint. Active listening is an acquired skill similar to learning to be an effective speaker. It also helps the supervisor/manager to gauge how the employee is reacting to the situation. Listening gives the employee an opportunity to vent, to release pent-up frustrations. Skillful, active listening, along with encouraging the employee

to explain the situation in detail and from different viewpoints, often results in a better understanding of the situation and an appropriate response to it on the part of the employee. Such discussions can elicit positive solutions that the employee may not have otherwise thought of. The manager should let the employee know that her or his own ability to develop positive solutions to resolve the issue is respected and appreciated.

4. Help the employee(s) identify the specific steps needed to solve the problem. Set specific objectives for the employee to meet and help the person to devise a specific action plan for meeting these objectives. The manager may need to provide coaching or counseling to make it possible for the employee to succeed in these objectives. If so, these steps also should be discussed in detail in order that each side may know exactly what is expected.

5. Follow up with increased surveillance of the situation to ensure that the employee is making effort and satisfactory progress according to the plan. Many plans to solve problems fall apart because the supervisor fails to monitor the results. Sometimes the supervisor thinks the employee will automatically change the behavior because they have talked about it. In other situations, the supervisor simply forgets to follow up. If the employee's progress is not monitored, the employee may feel that the supervisor is not serious about the action plan they agreed upon. Coaching an employee by providing feedback regarding performance on a day-to-day basis helps both the employee and the supervisor.

Coaching

A most effective form of discipline is positive feedback and reinforcement. Do not mix positive feedback and reinforcement with negative criticism. With mixed signals, employees will become confused and will not be sure what is expected. They then usually resort to their old behaviors or do nothing. Any positive behaviors, even if they fail, should be reinforced with positive feedback and at least some form of external and/or internal reinforcement.

Do not use silence as feedback to positive behaviors. Too often managers assume that employees think that if they do not hear otherwise, they are doing alright. Silence can be interpreted in too many ways. In most cases, it will be perceived either as a negative gesture and/or as a lack of interest on the part of the manager.

Negative Discipline

It is not suggested that all negative discipline is undesirable. On the contrary, in some situations it is necessary. The trick is to know when and how. Negative discipline should be used as a last resort after employing the positive discipline techniques.

Negative discipline is most often employed by managers in authoritarian organizations. This approach is premised upon the belief that punishment is the formula for the correction of all behaviors, whatever the motive. The emotional tone of a disciplinary meeting is too often the expression of the manager's anger and irrational or inappropriate punishment or threats. If the manager intends to make the employee an example to dissuade other employees from similar behaviors, the situation is aggravated even further. Being made an example is demeaning to the employee. To some, such managerial behaviors are interpreted as provocative injustices, and the employee begins to feel like a victim entitled to retribution.

The following are some suggestions for administering negative discipline:

1. Never discipline an employee until all of the facts of the matter have been determined. The burden of proof is on management.
2. Although some organizations defer discipline to a human resources department, such a practice is undesirable. Even though it may seem that this removes the manager from the interpersonal aspect of the disciplinary process, that viewpoint is illusory. The supervisor must be personally responsible for administering negative discipline as well as positive discipline. In extreme cases, when prior discipline has been administered and this instance is going to be the last before it becomes necessary to terminate, another manager, often from human resources, may be present. Otherwise, negative discipline must always be administered in private by the employee's direct supervisor. Although obvious, this cardinal rule is often violated, and the consequences can be profound.
3. Inform the employee of the effects of the violation on company operations and co-workers.
4. State clearly and explicitly what constituted the unacceptable behavior.
5. Permit an explanation from the employee.
6. Make the discipline commensurate with the violation.
7. Explain the sanctions that will result from repeated behavior.
8. If the employee is experiencing external stressors that have contributed to the behavior and/or which will make it difficult for the employee to conform, refer the person to counseling by internal Employee Assistance Program provisions.

If the employee does not respond, then termination may be necessary. If so, follow the procedures set forth in the section entitled Layoff and Termination Procedures in this chapter.

Security Procedures

The previously cited Society for Human Resource Management survey found that 71% of respondents indicated their organizations had no policies for preventing or responding to violence in the workplace, and 69% said they had no plans to institute any.

An obvious strategy to help reduce or prevent potential violence is to impose stricter security measures in the organization. However, in many organizations undergoing downsizing, security is being downsized too. Some organizations do not employ security measures during working hours, and security measures after regular working hours may only consist of sporadic checks. A great number of organizations have no security measures at all. Even when there is security, ease of access and surprise rendered it ineffective against incidents of violence by employees of the host organization, as seen in some of the examples of incidents previously cited.

However, organizations must attempt to take all reasonable measures possible to prevent or at least inhibit violence on their premises. Some suggestions for enhancing premises security follow:

1. Employ a panic button for secretaries and receptionists to warn security and/or law enforcement agencies of a threatening or violent situation. This panic button should not be directly connected to a telephone switchboard because of the possibility of the assailant destroying the switchboard. Such a situation occurred in the Elgar Corporation in San Diego, California. The attacker destroyed the switchboard, seriously inhibiting employees' attempts to summon help.

2. Conduct training for all employees regarding the typologies of behavior common to violent people or precedent to violent behavior. Receptionists or doorkeepers in particular should be instructed regarding

behaviors and criteria by which to determine when help should be summoned.

3. Use restricted entry devices to premises. The following devices are common:
   - Magnetic identification card keys to door locks
   - Video monitoring of all outside entry doors from a nearby security office
   - Video monitoring of remote areas not normally patrolled by security personnel
   - A metal detector at all outside entry doors that will sound a warning in the security office
   - A sign-in procedure for all nonemployees or former employees; if entrance is granted, a guest must wear a guest badge in plain sight at all times
   - Picture identification cards worn in plain sight at all times by all active employees
   - A security officer at all unlocked outside doors
   - Bullet-proof or shatter-proof glass in doors and windows of offices near entrances to premises.
   - An alarm and/or a PA system to warn employees of critical events

Creating a Crisis Management Plan for Violent Events

In addition to taking steps to reduce potential violence, a plan must be created for action when violence does occur. A Crisis Management Team (CMT) and a Personnel Crisis Center should be created to develop crisis plans for each specific plant or location.

The Personnel Crisis Center should consist of one specific telephone number in each personnel or human resources office to receive all reports of threats, intimidation, and minor altercations and reports of typological behaviors of potentially violent people. The center should

create the rules and regulations concerning the reporting requirements of employees; the prohibitions against
making threats, harassing or intimidating other employees, or exhibiting violence of any kind; and the sanctions
for violation of these rules and regulations. The center
must create specific action plans and appropriate guidelines for the proactive and reactive responses to any events,
including any employee assistance plans and disciplinary and termination procedures. The center should play
a significant role in the development and administration
of the organization's past performance appraisal/evalua-
tion system. The coordinator of that center must take
affirmative action as appropriate and document com-
pletely all incidents and consequent responses. The coordinator of the crisis center should be a member of the
CMT.

The CMT, which may be synonymous with the Risk
Management Team, should develop a specific action plan
for response to a critical event of workplace violence.

The CMT should consist of:

- The top manager at the location
- The security manager
- The human resources manager and the coordinator of
  the Personnel Crisis Center
- Media-relations personnel
- General counsel
- Maintenance personnel

A crisis management plan should include:

1. **Telephones and/or emergency alarm buttons**—At
   frequent locations around the premises, particularly
   near the main entrances to the premises, employees
   should have access to, and familiarity with, locations
   of telephones and emergency alarm buttons. Employees usually are familiar with such locations in their
   own work areas, but should be familiar with those in
   other areas as well. Such devices should ring into the

security control panel or into the local authority 911 emergency dispatch center.

2. **Response capability**—If the organization has its own security force, all members of it should be familiar with the floor plans of the buildings that they protect and the most direct route from one point to another. If there is no organizational security and the premises are large or complex, the premises should be sectioned off in physical designations identified on doors and corridors so that responding authorities unfamiliar with the premises can locate the critical location quickly. This is also true for other emergency responses.

3. **Containment**—If a violent act can be contained to a small area, the potential for injury or loss of life may be minimized. For general security as well, the premises should be physically divided by security doors which, while not guarded, may be locked at night or during emergencies, limiting unauthorized access to smaller areas.

4. **Evacuation**—Evacuation plans for fire emergencies may serve for other emergencies as well, such as violent attacks. Fire and violent weather drills should be practiced and enforced on a regular basis.

5. **Local law enforcement agencies**—The CMT and/or security personnel should establish liaison with local law enforcement agencies, inviting them to tour the premises for familiarity and to secure additional suggestions for CMT interests.

6. **Liaison**—If violence should occur, a senior manager, as a member of the CMT, should be prepared to take charge of internal activities and act as liaison with emergency personnel. He or she should be assisted by the public relations officer, also a member of the CMT, who will act to inform employees, family members, and the press as appropriate.

7. **Hostage training**—All employees should be briefed as to how to act in the event they should be taken as a hostage.

8. **First aid training**—In addition to security personnel, a significant number of employees at all levels of the organization should be trained in first aid and cardiopulmonary resuscitation (CPR). Obviously, such preparations also are applicable in various other emergency situations.
9. **Post-event**—The CMT should provide for various functions following the termination of emergency events:
   * Counseling of victims, witnesses, customers, and family members
   * Emergency safety inspections of premises for electrical, gas, or other hazardous potentials
   * Clean-up
   * Repairs

An incident at Fairchild Air Force Base in Spokane, Washington, involved a former airman who returned to the base hospital with an assault rifle and, in a shooting spree, killed 4 people and wounding another 23. A multiagency emergency plan was instituted and, as best as possible under the circumstances, worked as planned.

Hostage Behavior Training

Employees should be trained how to act so as to maximize survival potential if taken hostage. It is not unusual for a violent event to develop into a hostage situation. A case in point is one example cited in Chapter 2, wherein John Wayne Burns entered the overhead door business and took an employee hostage. There have been quite a number of other situations in which multiple hostages were taken and, in some cases, held for significant periods and released. In other cases, employees and/or customers were killed by the hostage taker.

When the person targeted for violence was not available, in some cases the assailant has taken one or more hostages, either in lieu of the intended target or to demand that the target be brought to the location. This happened in California, where a former telephone company employee took hostages. In another instance, hostages were taken in an apartment complex clubhouse, and the hostage taker demanded that his boss be brought to him.

If employees should be taken hostage, there are no behaviors that guarantee survival. However, some hostage behaviors have been found to increase the odds of survival more often than not:

- Do not argue with the hostage taker over any issue, particularly about the propriety of his behavior or the reasons for it.
- Do not separate or set yourself against the person logically or emotionally. Even though you most naturally would feel this way, the more closely you can relate to his plight, the better chance you have of establishing a rapport with him. If you become valued, you have a better chance he will not want to hurt you.
- Do not appear to be unemotional or uninvolved. Some men feel that their macho is measured according to how "cool" they are under pressure. In such instances, the more positive emotional exchange there is between the hostage and perpetrator, the better for the hostage.
- Engage in conversation with the perpetrator to the degree he will permit, and talk about personal hopes, fears, weaknesses, family, and other matters that build your identity as a real person instead of just "a person." Even ask his advice if he will permit. Focus on the future in conversation and on your hopes to be with your family. Make these hopes very modest; do not focus on your career.
- Gently encourage him to refer to you by your nickname.

- To the degree that he wishes to talk with you, encourage him to do so. Be a sympathetic and sincere listener. If he identifies his antagonist, or original target, sympathize with his viewpoint and identification as a victim, but only if he obviously has no access or hope of access to that person during the event.

- Do not try to "reason" with him, to defend the company or even yourself, should you be the actual target. He is fully committed to his position. You usually are better off agreeing and, if you *are* his antagonist, becoming repentant for having had poor judgment in dealing with him. Be sincere. He is most resentful of your authority, how you used it, and your insensitivity to his interests. He now wishes to show you how it feels to have power exercised over you and retribution exacted. Do not willingly grovel, but be very remorseful, empathetic, and respectful. Do not tell him that you understand how he feels, because he knows that you cannot. You can attempt to empathize or appreciate how he must feel and acknowledge justification of his feelings.

- Do not be condescending in any way. It was his perception of your misuse of power that very likely has fueled his anger and resentment. He now feels he is in power. Condescension, at this point, could be fatal.

- Do not be self-righteous in any way. As far as you are concerned, his viewpoint that he is justified in his behavior should not be challenged; there is not room for two being self-righteous. He will not permit it unless you share an antagonist, which he might permit.

- Do not give the impression you think he will fail or that it is hopeless for him to think he will succeed in what he is doing—*or* that you expect the situation to come out alright. You must permit him to view himself to be current master of your fate, and he well may be.

- Do not watch him all of the time. It makes it appear that you are on guard and defensive. Make it appear that you are submitting to his control and his mercy.
- Do be subservient and agree there is much unfairness in the world, that people should not push each other around or treat each other unfairly. Become some kind of similar victim yourself. If he permits you to tell about it, do so, but do not let your story become more important than or even compete with his.
- Side with him in all matters and join with him against the authorities, but don't oversell it. Make yourself a "victim" of the organization too (not a special person).
- Carefully test the permitted range of movement while engendering trust and exhibiting dependency on him.
- Remember the true situation and realize the authorities may need your help at some point to help you.
- Although some of these actions may be against one's nature, or may even be deceptive and distasteful, remember that the idea is to survive.

Handling Reports of Threats

An organization and its managers have significant duties and legal obligations to make sure they have taken reasonable measures to prevent violence in the workplace. The federal Occupational Safety and Health Administration (OSHA) requires employers to provide employees a safe and healthy workplace. That includes reasonable efforts to protect them from each other. Since the next perpetrator of violence probably is already in the workplace, a policy for reporting threats should be developed. This policy will allow anyone in the organization who has information about a specific threat to report it to the proper organization officials.

Threat reports should be handled in the following manner:

- Company rules should dictate that any threat by an employee should be reported promptly to both the supervisor and to the human resources department. A supervisor/manager may discount the threat and not report it any further. In this manner, at least two people have been put on notice of the problem, doubling the potential of its being taken seriously. The person reporting the threat must be interviewed to determine:
  - o The exact nature of the threat
  - o The specific circumstances in which the threat was made
  - o The relationship between the person reporting the threat and the person making the threat
  - o The names of any witnesses who heard the threat, witnessed the incident which caused the threat, or have knowledge of other threats made by the person in the past
- An investigation should be conducted to determine the veracity of the threat report. The investigation should be conducted in a discreet manner; any interviews conducted with witnesses must be kept confidential and thoroughly documented. Legal counsel should be consulted if there is a question about how the investigation should be conducted. There is a possibility that the employee reporting the threat has done so to get back at another employee. The reporter may even be the original antagonist.
- An assessment of the severity of the threat should be made. Sometimes this is difficult to do. If there are questions about the severity and potential for realization, outside professional help should be consulted before final determinations are made as to what actions are required.

There is a note of caution in attempting to predict accurately the potential for violent behavior. In 1981, John Monahan, a noted author and expert on the prediction of violent behavior, stated, "All a person predicting violence can hope to do is assign a probability figure to the occurrence of violent behavior by a given individual during a given time period." If this is the case, the question is, "What does the assessed degree of probability recommend in the way of prevention?"

If there is sufficient probability to believe that the threat is valid, a specific plan of action must be developed in response. Such a plan must include the protection of the person who has been threatened and/or the person reporting the threat. If the person making the threat learns that someone has reported him, the reporter also may be identified as an antagonist.

In some instances, protection may need to be extended beyond the workplace. In that event, law enforcement authorities must be informed of the situation. If the employee's plan to carry out his threat at work is frustrated by additional security measures, he may choose to carry it out outside the premises of the employer. If the matter has advanced to this stage, it is most likely that the employee will be terminated, at which time the primary responsibility for further response primarily lies with the law enforcement authorities. The potential for the employee re-entering the employer's premises is significant, and the CMT contingency plans for such an event must be in place.

The obligation of the employer to warn other employees when a fellow employee has been assessed to be potentially violent is governed by morality and by law to the extent that the employer must provide that safe workplace. Employers fear that since threat assessments are not 100% scientific and accurate, identifying employees, now former employees, as threats could leave them vulnerable to lawsuits from those individuals. Consequently, employers are reluctant to do so. On the other hand, if an event does in fact occur, failing to warn employees leaves employers vulnerable to lawsuits from any victims. Also, if an employee is discharged because of accusations of violent tendencies, the employee may sue for wrongful discharge. Therefore, actual incidents or threats of misconduct must be fully documented.

Whether or not any organization has prepared to handle an act of violence, it will be forced to do so if one occurs. The CMT must address the extent to which management, other employees, and, in particular, security guards are authorized to act in response beyond self-preservation. Once law enforcement responds, organizational personnel are cast into supporting roles, but the nature of their first-response behaviors likely will impact the nature of succeeding events.

Dispute-Resolution Training

All managers and employees should be given training in dispute-resolution techniques, not only for the prevention of violence, but also for day-to-day interpersonal interactions that transpire in the workplace. Americans have a cultural norm of idealizing the competitive individual and a win–lose philosophy about conflict. However, much research and experience in the field over the last 50 years have revealed that there are tactics that can be employed toward the positive resolution of interpersonal and intergroup conflict with a win–win approach. The trick, however, is for at least one of the disputants to understand and know how to employ these tactics. Should both parties in dispute have these skills, the potential for positive resolution significantly increases.

Conflict among people is a natural phenomenon. However, the two most popular approaches are to avoid confrontation or to confront to win. In fact, since conflict is common in everyone's life, it actually is an opportunity to solve the root problem. Avoidance leaves the problem intact to magnify in proportion until it may become unmanageable, left to an unavoidable, desperate, and destructive finale. People who are skilled in dispute resolution are able to confidently broach a problem with an attitude of collaboration and compromise. Obviously, positive solution to problems is both constructive and cathartic.

Dispute-resolution training does not require a large investment of time or money. A ten-hour block of training is probably a minimum, but in that time the most significant elements of the dynamics and tactics of conflict and the tenets of "integrative bargaining," or win–win negotiation, can be explained.

The Aftermath

Although workplace violence is not a pleasant subject, it must be addressed, and a plan must be in place. The CMT should have a contingency plan for the company's role in the aftermath. The following are considerations for the particulars of such a plan:

1. Obviously, the first consideration is to provide medical attention.
2. Either shut down the company until normal operations can be fully restored, or isolate the area and resume normal operations in the remainder of the organization.
3. Provide for immediate counseling for all employees who wish to accept it. Contact the community crisis center that has been designated by the CMT to intervene in such a situation.

In a 1991 study conducted by the Barrington Institute in Los Angeles, California, 200 people who were suffering from major psychological trauma were followed during recovery. Half of these people were provided therapy immediately after the traumatic event, and the other half began therapy sometime later. The study found that the first group averaged 12 weeks of recovery time before returning to work, and the second group had an average recovery time of 46 weeks.

Many people who suffer significant psychological trauma develop post-traumatic stress disorder (PTSD). Those who receive early counseling are better equipped to deal with PTSD and work through its stages more quickly. According to the *Diagnostic and Statistical Manual of Mental Disorders–IV,* a person with PTSD has been exposed to a traumatic event in which both of the following were present:

1. The person experienced, witnessed, or was confronted with an event or events that involved actual or threatened death or serious injury, or a threat to the physical integrity of self or others.
2. The person's response involved intense fear, helplessness, or horror.

In PTSD, the following symptoms are common:

- The traumatic event is persistently re-experienced
- Persistent avoidance of stimuli associated with the trauma
- Persistent symptoms of increased arousal (not present before the trauma), as indicated by at least two of the following:
  - Difficulty falling asleep or staying asleep
  - Irritability or outbursts of anger
  - Difficulty concentrating
  - Hypervigilance
  - An exaggerated startle response
  - A physiologic reactivity on exposure to events that symbolize or resemble an aspect of the traumatic event

The disorder is considered acute if the duration is less than three months and is considered chronic if the duration is longer than three months. For some individuals suffering from PTSD, the traumatic event remains for decades, in some cases for their whole lifetime. It is a dominating psychological experience that has the power to evoke panic, terror, grief, or despair that will be manifested as daytime fantasies, nightmares, and flashbacks. Sufferers may experience an effect known as "psychic numbing," an emotional anesthesia that makes it difficult for them to participate in meaningful interpersonal relationships.

Personal psychological counseling helps an individual to examine personal values and how he or she was violated during the traumatic event. The goal of the counseling is the resolution of the conscious and unconscious conflicts that were created by the event. The individual also has to work to rebuild self-esteem, self-control, and renew a sense of pride and integrity.

Other facts and statistics about the after-effects of violence support the need for immediate counseling:

- One hundred percent of the victims of violence report major changes in either their lives or their families' lives following the event.
- Traumatized employees of violence will likely be substantially less productive after the incident.
- About 200,000 new cases of PTSD occur each year, with related costs of approximately $100 billion annually.
- There are predictable phases of recovery that victims of workplace violence go through.
- The severity of the response to witnessing or experiencing violence is affected by the length of the incident and how much warning there was prior to the incident.
- After a violent experience, most victims feel vulnerable and feel that no place is safe for them.

The organization is responsible for notifying the families of any victims of injury or death. As unpleasant as this task is, it must be done. The organization also provides for any necessary support the members of the family might need. This could include counseling, financial help, or other arrangements. The crisis center should be used to help determine the best method for this task.

As soon as possible, the CMT should prepare to do the following:

- Prepare a statement for the media addressing what has occurred in the organization. Be prepared to respond to a broad range of questions. With the apparent increase in the frequency of violence in the workplace, most media reporters are certain to have many penetrating questions. Responsible answers will displace the necessity for the media to seek information from other less reliable sources and minimize the creation of false information, which, if reported, could be damaging to all involved. If the CMT or company spokesperson cannot legally or ethically respond to some question, they should not attempt to hedge, but simply indicate that he or she cannot answer the question.
- Informational meetings for all employees should be set up to keep them informed about what happened and what now is happening. Also, employees must be informed that the company has a plan in operation for helping everyone through the situation. These meetings should be held as often as possible to keep employees informed. If necessary, a hot-line should be set up to answer questions of employees who are not at work or who are on different shifts.
- The CMT should have defined the roles of each level of company management for the aftermath. They will undoubtedly be asked questions by employees or other interested parties and should have accurate, current information with which to keep their own subordinates informed.

- The CMT should initiate investigation of what occurred in order to improve emergency contingency plans, if possible. Even though law enforcement agencies will investigate the incident, an independent internal investigation should be launched immediately to determine all of the circumstances surrounding the violent act.

Even though the company may have provided for individual and group counseling, those employees directly involved, and even some not directly involved but who were friends of those who were, may take some time to return to "normal." Managers should realize that:

- Employees may not immediately return to "business as usual."
- Employees may not be "rational" about the violent incident.
- Employees may not perform at the same level of performance as before the incident.

Training for Supervisors/Managers

For the most part, supervisors/managers are unaware of the specific circumstances under which an individual and the workplace interact to produce the potential for violent actions. Training should be developed to help them recognize and respond to these potentially dangerous situations. Topics that should be included in this training are:

- **Stress**—The ability to recognize excess distress in employees, how to help them handle it, and how to eliminate its sources.
- **Interpersonal relationships**—Skills that are necessary to be effective in positively interacting with people from a position of authority.

1. *Listening skills*—These are the skills that enable a person to really listen, not just hear, and understand what another person is saying. Listening is an active process, not a passive one. It is an art too few people, particularly managers, have developed. Skills also include ways of responding so other people feel their problems and feelings have been understood and are important.
2. *Assertion skills*—These are the verbal and nonverbal behaviors that enable people to maintain the respect they need but at the same time not dominate, manipulate, abuse, or control other people.
3. *Conflict-management skills*—Managers must understand that conflict is a normal and healthy situation that occurs between people in organizations. These skills enable a person to deal with conflict in a positive way that results in the solution of the core problem to the satisfaction of all parties involved. Emotional turbulence often accompanies conflict. But the ability to work toward the positive resolution of conflict tends to pacify the emotions because it restores some sense of control and positive expectation instead of negative expectation. The knowledge of the different conflict strategies, and when to use them, empowers people, and they find that working through conflict often forges a closer relationship between the parties after the conflict is over.
4. *Handling difficult people*—Managers must know how to intervene and deal positively with dysfunctional behavior in the workplace. They must recognize when employees are exhibiting excessive frustrations or hostility and when to make appropriate referrals if they believe employees to be at risk.

- **Roles**—Learning the different roles of employee assistance professionals, security management, medical personnel, human resources, and other support resource personnel.

- **Addressing harassment of employees**—People have the capacity to harass others on myriad different bases. Managers must address these problems and ensure fair treatment of all employees.
- **Disciplining employees**—How to effectively discipline employees.
- **Performance appraisal skills**—These skills are necessary for making good performance appraisals.

For the training of managers to be effective, it must be directly linked to their real working environments and conducted by professionals with experience.

Summary

Violence in the workplace has become a common social phenomenon. Where and when it will happen is difficult, but not impossible, to predict. Although there are no absolutes in human behavior, we can learn to detect indicators of discontent. We can develop contingency action plans with preventive measures. We can develop measures to inhibit violent behavior. We can "harden" access to our premises, even access by employees. We can respond more effectively and efficiently when violence occurs. We can be prepared to pick up the pieces and put them back together with greater skill than we have in the past. All organizations should have a CMT to prepare plans to achieve all of these things. Most organizations have neither a CMT nor such plans. Most do not even see the need for them.

This book is meant to encourage those reluctant organizations and convince them they should develop a crisis management plan. At first glance, most organizations figure the cost–benefit ratio is unfavorable to making such an investment in time, money, and effort. However, one instance can make the investment worthwhile, and the odds are that incidents, albeit small ones, indeed will occur in those workplaces. Most of the measures set forth above even pay off for organizations in handling "minor" incidents by reducing discord in everyday work relationships. In doing so, they may be precluding the "major" event, but such abstract analysis and logic is too much of a long shot for many managers who evaluate and decide in immediate perspectives. A well-thought-out plan may save an organization the pain, suffering, and costs exemplified in many of the cases cited. Organizations want a stable, healthy, productive workplace where employees can feel free to apply their skills. All can achieve this goal, if they care to do so.

REFERENCES

Allport, Gordon W., *Personality: A Psychological Interpretation* (Harry Holt and Company, New York), 1937.

Anfuso, Dawn, "Violence-Prevention Strategies Limit Legal Liabilities," *Personnel Journal*, Vol. 73, Issue 10, Oct. 1994.

Anfuso, Dawn, "Deflecting Workplace Violence," *Personnel Journal*, Vol. 73, Issue 10, Oct. 1994.

Anonymous, "Reducing Violence in the Workplace," *Supervisory Management*, Vol. 39, June 1994.

Anonymous, "Preemployment Screening, Recommendations, Hiring, Negligence," *Small Business Reports*, Vol. 18, Issue 7, July 1993.

Associated Press, "Suspect in Professor's Shooting Kills Himself," *Chicago Daily Herald*, March 11, 1995, Section 7, p. 1.

Associated Press, "Co-worker Held in Shooting that Killed 2 in Cereal Plant."

Associated Press, "3 Die, 6 Wounded in Michigan Post Office Shooting," *Washington Post,* Nov. 15, 1991, p. A-3.

Baltimore Sun, "Murders Cause 40 Percent of Deaths of Women in Workplace, Survey Says," Oct. 2, 1993, p. A-3.

Baron, S. Anthony, *Violence in the Workplace* (Pathfinder Publishing of California, Ventura, CA), 1993.

Bensimon, Helen Frank, "Violence in the Workplace," *Training and Development,* Vol. 48, No. 1, Jan. 1994.

Billiter, Bill, "Post Office Shootings Reflect Stress in the Workplace," *Los Angeles Times—Washington Edition,* May 7, 1993 p. A-7.

Boxell, Bettina, Eric Malnic, and Jeff Leeds, "City Worker Held after 4 Supervisors Are Slain," *Los Angeles Times,* July 20, 1995, p. A-1.

Branch, Walton J., "Dealing with Dangerous Employees," *Security Management,* Vol. 37, No. 9, Sept. 1993, p. 81.

Burdick, Thomas, "Violence in the Workplace Is on the Rise," *Washington Times,* Sept. 2, 1993, p. C-2.

Bureau of Labor Statistics, "Workplace Homicides in 1992," *Compensation and Working Conditions,* U.S. Department of Labor, Feb. 1994.

Castelli, Jim, "On-the-Job Violence Becomes Epidemic" (report by National Institute of Occupational Safety and Health), *Safety and Health,* Vol. 149, No. 2, Feb. 1994.

Causey, Mike, "The Federal Diary: Post Office Security," *Washington Post,* June 16, 1992, p. B-2.

Cawood, James, "On the Edge: Assessing the Violent Employee," *Security Management*, Sept. 1991.

Corsini, Raymond J., Editor, *Encyclopedia of Psychology*, Vols. 1, 2, 3 (John Wiley and Sons), 1994.

Cotliar, Sharon and Phillip J. O'Connor, "Old Grudge Blamed in NU Prof's Shooting," *Chicago Sun-Times*, March 10, 1995, p. 1.

Criminal Victimization in the United States, 1992: A National Crime Victimization Survey Report, U.S. Department of Justice, NCJ, Washington, D.C.

Diagnostic and Statistical Manual of Mental Disorders, IV (American Psychiatric Association, Washington, D.C.), 1994.

Dollard, J., N. Miller, L. Doob, O.H. Mowrer, and R.R. Sears, *Frustration and Aggression* (Yale University Press, New Haven, CT), 1939.

Dreyer, R.S., "Fired for Cause," *Supervision*, Vol. 55, No. 9, Sept. 1994.

Edwards, Sherri, "Woman Held as Hostage a 2nd Time," *The Indianapolis Star*, Jan. 25, 1995, p. D-1.

Felsentahl, Edward, "Potentially Violent Employees Present Bosses with a Catch-22," *Wall Street Journal*, April 5, 1995, p. B-1.

Fox, James Alan, "Postal Violence: Cycle of Despair Turns Tragic," *USA Today*, May 12, 1993, p. A-13.

Friend, Daniel C. "Safeguarding Your Staff," *Security Management*, Vol. 34, No. 6, June 1990, p. 57.

Graham, James P., "Disgruntled Employees—Ticking Time Bombs," *Security Management*, Jan. 1992.

Greenwood, Joan, "Companies See More Workplace Violence," *Wall Street Journal*, April 4, 1994 p. B-1.

Hodgson, Karyn, "Positive Steps for Screening Out Workplace Violence," *Security*, Vol. 31, No. 1, Jan. 1994, p. 67.

Hodgson, Karyn, "Culture Clash: USPS Redefines Hiring/Training Policies," *Security*, Vol. 30, No. 7, July 1993, p. 45.

Inwald, Robin, "Those Seven Deadly Sins," *Security Management*, Vol. 34, No. 4, April 1990, p. 73.

Jimenez, Gilbert, "NU Shooting Suspect Kills Self at Minn. Dean's Office," *Chicago Sun-Times*, March 11, 1995, p. 1.

Johnson, Dennis L., "A Team Approach to Threat Assessment," *Security Management*, Vol. 38, No. 9, Sept. 1994.

Johnson, Michelle Laque, "Some Guidelines on Checking, and Giving, References," *Investor's Daily*, July 19, 1991, p. 8.

Kurland, Orin M., "Workplace Violence," *Risk Management*, Vol. 40, No. 6, June 1993, p. 76.

Larson, Erik, "Trigger Happy, A False Crisis: How Workplace Violence Became a Hot Issue," *Wall Street Journal*, Oct. 13, 1994, p. A-1.

Lawlor, Julia, "Survey: Homicides at Work on the Rise," *USA Today*, Oct. 18, 1993, p. B-3.

Lawlor, Julia, "Executives on Guard Against Violence," *USA Today,* Aug. 18, 1993, p. B-1.

Lewis, Robert, "Downsizing Taking a Higher Toll," *AARP Bulletin,* Vol. 35, No. 10, Nov. 1994.

Lissy, William, E., "Workplace Violence," *Supervision,* Vol. 55, No. 4, April 1994.

Lundin, Robert W., *Personality: An Experimental Approach* (MacMillan and Co., New York), 1961.

Marks, Peter, "A New Worry: Going to Work Can Be Murder," *New York Times,* Feb. 25, 1993, p. B-1.

Marovic, Milan, "The Right Way to Rightsize," *Industry Week,* Sept. 5, 1994, p. 46.

McAllister, Bill, "Runyon Vows Efforts to Curb Violence at Post Offices," *Washington Post,* Aug. 6, 1993, p. A-19.

McCune, Jenny C., "Companies Grapple with Workplace Violence," *Management Review,* Vol. 83, No. 3, March, 1994.

Megargee, E., "The Prediction of Dangerous Behavior," *Criminal Justice and Behavior,* Vol. 3, 1976.

Monahan, John, "The Causes of Violence," *FBI Law Enforcement Bulletin,* Jan. 1994.

Monahan, John, *Predicting Violent Behavior: An Assessment of Clinical Techniques* (Sage Publications, Beverly Hills, CA), 1981.

Nomani, Asra Q., "Murder Is High among Causes of Deaths at Work" (Labor Department's 2nd National Census of

Fatal Occupational Injuries), *Wall Street Journal,* Aug. 11, 1994, p. A-4.

Northwestern National Life Insurance Co., *Fear and Violence in the Workplace,* 1993.

O'Boyle, Thomas F., "Disgruntled Workers Intent on Revenge Increasingly Harm Colleagues and Bosses," *Wall Street Journal,* Sept. 15, 1992, p. B-1.

Pack, Susan, "Fatal Firings," *Baltimore Sun–Maryland Business Weekly,* March 16, 1992 p. 4.

Prince, John J., "Fuming over Workplace Violence," *Security Management,* Vol. 37, No. 3, Jan. 1993, p. 64.

Purdy, Matthew, "Workplace Murders Provoke Lawsuits and Better Security," *New York Times,* Feb. 14, 1994, p. A-1.

Rigdon, Joan E., "Companies See More Workplace Violence" (American Management Association survey), *Wall Street Journal,* April 12, 1994, p. B-1.

Rosen, Mark, "Prescreen to Avoid Getting Burned," *Security Management,* Vol. 37, No. 4; April 1993, p. 38.

Selye, Hans, *Stress without Distress* (J.B. Lippincott, New York), 1974.

Selye, Hans, *The Stress of Life* (McGraw-Hill, New York), 1956.

Shafer, David J., "Eli Lilly Ready to Defend Prosac in Trial," *The Indianapolis Star,* Sept. 25, 1994, p. E-1.

Silverstein, Stuart, "Stalked by Violence on the Job. Domestic Violence and Abuse Is Spilling Over into the Workplace," *Los Angeles Times,* Aug. 8, 1994, p. A-1.

Simon, Stephanie and Paul Feldman, "Search Goes on for Answers to Violence in the Workplace," *Los Angeles Times,* July 30, 1995, p. B-1.

Solomon, Jolie, "Waging War in the Workplace," *Newsweek,* Vol. 122, No. 3, July 19, 1993, p. 30.

Soloman, Mark B., "Study Says Stress at UPS Could Provoke Violence," *Journal of Commerce*, June 4, 1993, p. B-3.

Stearman, Brian, "Workers Subdued after Tragedy," *Marion Chronicle-Tribune,* Sept. 1, 1994, p. A-7.

Stearman, Brian and Bob Musinski, "Husband Flees, Kills Self Later at Home," *Marion Chronicle-Tribune,* Aug. 31, 1994.

Stuart, Peggy, "Murder on the Job," *Personnel Journal,* Feb. 1992, pp. 72–84.

Suplee, Curt, "Berserk," *Washington Post,* Oct, 1, 1991, p. D-1.

Sweetland, Richard and Daniel Keeper, *Tests—A Comprehensive Reference for Assessments in Psychology, Education, and Business,* 3rd edition (Pro-Ed, Austin, TX), 1991.

Swoboda, Frank, "Increasingly the Shadow of Violence Hangs Over U.S. Workers," *Washington Post,* Jan. 2, 1994, p. H-2.

Toufexis, Anastasia, "Workers Who Fight Firing with Fire," *Time,* Vol. 143, April 25, 1994.

Tremi, William, B., "Wife Chased Armed Teacher to School—Arrived after Shooting," *Ann Arbor News,* Aug. 6, 1994, p. A-1.

Wiggins, James A., Beverly B. Wiggins, and James VanderZanden, *Social Psychology,* 5th edition (McGraw-Hill, New York), 1994.

Williams, Tedra T., "Today's Workers Increasingly Put Under Microscope," *The Indianapolis Star,* Feb. 19, 1995, p. E-7.

Windsor, Patricia, "Students' Picture of Leith Mixed," *Ann Arbor News,* Dec. 17, 1993, p. A-9.